BRIDGING REALMS

TRANSLATING YOUR NON-TECH SKILLS INTO GRC GOLD

Tolulope Michael

TABLE OF CONTENTS

CHAPTER THREE

PROFESSIONALS WHO CAN VENTURE INTO GRC

CHAPTER FOUR

DECODING GRC ESSENTIALS: A NON-TECH APPROACH

CHAPTER FIVE

IMPLEMENTING GRC TECHNOLOGIES

CHAPTER SIX

SUSTAINING EXCELLENCE:CONTINUOUS MONITORING AND IMPROVEMENT IN THE GRC ODYSSEY

CHAPTER SEVEN

CASE STUDIES AND BEST PRACTICES

CHAPTER EIGHT

THE SYNERGY OF COMMUNICATION - BUILDING BRIDGES IN GRC

CHAPTER NINE

STRATEGIC THINKING: THE CORNERSTONE OF GRC EXCELLENCE

CHAPTER TEN

FROM INSIGHT TO ACTION: LEVERAGING YOUR UNIQUE GRC SKILL SET

REFERENCES

ABOUT THE AUTHOR

INTRODUCTION

In an era defined by rapid technological evolution, the bridge between the realms of traditional skills and the dynamic landscape of Governance, Risk, and Compliance (GRC) has never been more crucial. As organizations navigate the complex interplay of regulations, cybersecurity threats, and ethical considerations, the demand for professionals who can seamlessly translate non-tech skills into GRC gold has reached unprecedented heights.

"Bridging Realms: Translating Your Non-Tech Skills into GRC Gold" is a guide crafted for individuals who possess an arsenal of non-technical talents and are eager to harness them in the context of GRC. This book is a roadmap for those who understand the importance of compliance, risk management, and governance but may not be fluent in the language of technology. It illuminates the path for readers to not only survive but thrive in the realm where traditional expertise intersects with cutting-edge technologies and methodologies.

As we embark on this transformative journey, we will explore how individuals with backgrounds in diverse fields—ranging from finance and law to communication and psychology—can leverage their unique perspectives to fortify organizations against the ever-evolving challenges of the digital age. Whether you're a seasoned professional seeking to adapt to the demands of the modern workforce or a newcomer aspiring to make a mark in the GRC space, this book provides insights, strategies, and practical advice to empower you on your quest to turn your non-tech skills into GRC gold.

Join us as we traverse the realms, bridging the gap between the known and the unknown, and unlocking the doors to a future where the synergy of traditional expertise and technological prowess defines success in the world of Governance, Risk, and Compliance.

CHAPTER ONE

NAVIGATING THE GRC LANDSCAPE

Doing business is an age-long human endeavour that has witnessed many evolutions and developments across times and eras. This makes the landscape of business an ever-evolving one that is filled with intricacies, uncertainties and dynamics.

It is this attendant historical volatility that has necessitated solutions that will guarantee stability and solidity, one of which is a guiding framework known as Governance, Risk and Compliance (GRC). To paint a picture, GRC can be described as the conductor of an intricate symphony, seamlessly harmonizing the elements that define an organization's journey — governance steering the ship, risk navigating the turbulent waters, and compliance ensuring the voyage adheres to the rules of the vast regulatory sea.

On GRC, one of its experts and public figures, Michael Rasmussen, says that, "*GRC is a capability that enables an organisation to reliably achieve objectives while addressing uncertainty and acting with integrity.*"

As smooth as GRC sounds as an acronym, it is more than just that. It is a strategic framework, a compass, that directs organizations through the intricate blend of decision-making, risk mitigation, and adherence to regulatory. You could call it the invisible hand that shapes the destiny of businesses, ensuring they navigate the complex terrain with resilience, foresight, and a commitment to ethical and compliant conduct.

This symphony of GRC weaves together the threads of governance, where leadership sets the tone and charts the course; risk, where the unpredictable currents are met with strategic navigation; and compliance, where the organization dances in harmony with the legal and ethical rhythms that govern its industry. The result is not just a melodious ensemble but also a resilient and agile organization, capable of facing challenges head-on while staying attuned to the ever-changing cadence of the business world.

It is why this book exists – to serve as a bridge that will ease the transition of people with non-tech skills into GRC, making them invaluable in the process. This book will help you transtate your non-tech skills into gold in the realm of GRC. It also uncovers the nuances of effective governance, the artistry of risk management, and the compliance ballet that ensures businesses not only survive but thrive in a world where the only constant is change.

Again, welcome to the captivating overture of Governance, Risk, and Compliance — where strategic harmony meets the dynamic rhythm of the business realm. But how then do you navigate your way into the GRC landscape?

Let's start with the basics of expanding the basic concepts of GRC. But before then, it is important to reiterate that GRC forms a triad of essential elements that collectively shape the strategic direction, risk management practices, and compliance efforts within an organization. In an era characterized by complex regulatory environments, dynamic business landscapes, and increased stakeholder scrutiny, GRC emerges as a holistic framework that organizations adopt to navigate these challenges.

1.1 DEFINING GOVERNANCE

Governance refers to the set of structures, processes, and practices that guide, direct, and control an organization's activities. It involves defining responsibilities, establishing accountability, and ensuring that decision-making aligns with the organization's goals and values.

Governance in the context of Governance, Risk, and Compliance (GRC) is a comprehensive and multifaceted concept that forms the bedrock of organizational structure, decision-making processes, and ethical conduct. At its essence, governance refers to the framework of rules, policies, and practices that guide the actions and behaviors of individuals within an organization. It encompasses the distribution of responsibilities, the establishment of accountability, and the creation of mechanisms for decision-making that align with the organization's strategic objectives and values.

Also, governance serves as the overarching umbrella that sets the tone for risk management and compliance efforts. It is the mechanism through which an organization defines its purpose, establishes its mission, and formulates its long-term goals. Effective governance ensures that decision-making processes are transparent, ethical, and aligned with the interests of stakeholders, including shareholders, employees, and the broader community. GRC involves a range of issues covering internal and external information management and reporting. Good GRC enables an organization to keep its internal stakeholders (employees, contractors, consultants) informed, while also enabling smooth information exchange along the value chain of suppliers and customers(Quocirca, 2013).

One of the key components of governance is the establishment and composition of governing bodies such as boards of directors. These bodies play a pivotal role in shaping the strategic direction of the organization, overseeing executive leadership, and ensuring that risk management and compliance activities are integrated into the overall decision-making framework.

You should know that governance extends beyond formal structures and also involves the creation of a corporate culture that fosters accountability, transparency, and ethical behavior. It is about instilling a sense of responsibility and integrity throughout the organization, from top-level executives to front-line employees. This cultural aspect of governance is instrumental in promoting a risk-aware mindset and ensuring compliance with both external regulations and internal policies.

Where governance is effective, it inevitably becomes instrumental in creating an environment where risks are identified, assessed, and managed in a systematic manner. It establishes the parameters within which risk-taking is acceptable and ensures that risk management strategies align with the organization's overall goals.

In a nutshell, governance in GRC is a foundational element that encompasses the formal structures, decision-making processes, and cultural attributes that shape an organization. It serves as the guiding force that not only defines the organization's purpose and objectives but also establishes the principles for managing risks and ensuring compliance. A robust governance framework is indispensable for organizations seeking to navigate the complexities of the business landscape while upholding ethical standards and meeting the expectations of stakeholders.

1.2 Unpacking Risk Management

Risk, within the GRC context, involves the identification, assessment, and management of uncertainties that could impact the achievement of organizational objectives. It encompasses both threats and opportunities, requiring a proactive approach to risk mitigation and exploitation.

The second leg of the tripartite GRC is a pervasive and dynamic element that forms an integral part of organizational decision-making and strategic planning. It encapsulates the uncertainty surrounding potential events and outcomes, both positive and negative, that could impact an organization's ability to achieve its objectives. Understanding, managing, and mitigating risks are fundamental components of the GRC framework, enabling organizations to navigate uncertainties, capitalize on opportunities, and protect against potential threats.

Risk management is also about looking forward and anticipating potential risks as the next big critical situation may be an event that has never occurred before (Steinberg 79-80). Within the GRC terrain, risks manifest in various forms, each requiring unique strategies for identification, assessment, and mitigation:

1. **Financial Risk:**

   This encompasses market fluctuations, currency exchange rates, and economic variables, financial risk management is crucial for safeguarding an organization's fiscal health.

   Financial risk is undoubtedly a critical facet that represents the potential impact on an organization's fiscal health and stability. In GRC, financial risk encompasses diverse uncertainties and exposures that can influence the realization of financial objectives.

   Here some of the dimensions of financial risk:

   a. **Market risk**, a key element within GRC, encompasses the vulnerability to financial loss stemming from fluctuations in market variables like interest rates, currency exchange rates, commodity prices, and equity values. GRC leaders navigate the complexities of market risk, ensuring the organization is equipped to handle market dynamics impacting its financial positions and investments.

   b. **Credit risk**, another pivotal aspect, involves the potential financial loss due to the failure of a borrower or counterparty to meet financial obligations. GRC professionals diligently establish and uphold robust credit risk management frameworks, incorporating effective credit assessment procedures and vigilant monitoring mechanisms to mitigate the repercussions of credit defaults.

c. **Liquidity risk**, a crucial consideration in GRC, revolves around the potential inability of an organization to fulfill short-term financial obligations due to a shortage of cash or easily convertible assets. GRC measures focus on maintaining adequate liquidity and implementing contingency plans to address potential liquidity challenges, safeguarding the organization's financial stability.

d. **Operational risk** introduces the prospect of financial loss arising from inadequate or failed internal processes, systems, people, or external events. GRC leaders integrate operational risk assessments into their frameworks, identifying vulnerabilities and implementing controls to fortify the organization's financial integrity.

e. **Compliance risk** is associated with potential financial loss resulting from non-compliance with laws, regulations, industry standards, or internal policies. GRC leaders diligently ensure that compliance measures are robust, regularly updated, and effectively communicated, mitigating the financial consequences of non-compliance.

f. **Strategic risk**, a dimension of financial risk, involves the potential for financial loss arising from decisions or actions adversely impacting the organization's ability to achieve its strategic objectives. GRC frameworks strategically assess and address potential financial risks associated with pivotal decisions, aligning them with the organization's overarching goals.

g. **Financial reporting risk** pertains to the potential for inaccuracies or misstatements in financial reporting, posing risks of financial loss or damage to the organization's reputation. GRC professionals play a pivotal role in implementing controls and processes that guarantee the accuracy and transparency of financial reporting, reducing the risk of financial repercussions.

h. **Fraud risk** involves the potential for financial loss due to deceptive practices, misappropriation of assets, or fraudulent activities. GRC frameworks include measures to prevent, detect, and respond to fraud, safeguarding the organization against financial losses associated with fraudulent activities.

2. **Operational Risk:**

This arises from internal processes, systems, and external events, operational risk management focuses on identifying vulnerabilities and implementing measures to enhance resilience against disruptions.

It is akin to navigating the intricate currents of an organization's daily functions, presenting the potential for financial loss stemming from internal processes, systems, human factors, or external events. Unlike risks tied to markets or credit, operational risk is deeply embedded in the fabric of day-to-day activities, demanding vigilant attention within a comprehensive GRC framework.

You should think of operational risk as a multifaceted challenge, categorized into people risk (related to human actions or inactions), process risk (linked to internal processes), system risk (involving technology and information systems), and external risk (stemming from events beyond organizational control). It extends its influence across personnel, technology, and external factors that have the capacity to disrupt the normal flow of business operations.

Identifying and assessing operational risks involve a meticulous examination of vulnerabilities and weaknesses. Risk assessments weigh the likelihood and potential impact of these operational risks, encompassing both internal and external factors that might pose threats.

Mitigating operational risk is a strategic dance of implementing measures to reduce the likelihood and impact of potential risks. This involves strengthening internal controls, fortifying cybersecurity measures, training employees, and establishing contingency plans to address potential disruptions.

This makes technology a key player in managing operational risk. Organizations leverage technology solutions such as risk management software, cybersecurity tools, and business continuity planning systems to identify, monitor, and mitigate operational risks effectively.

Business continuity planning becomes a linchpin in operational risk management. Organizations develop and regularly test business continuity plans, ensuring the ability to sustain essential operations during and after disruptions, thereby mitigating the impact of operational risks.

Transparent reporting and communication channels are paramount. Establishing clear reporting mechanisms allows organizations to communicate identified risks, control measures, and mitigation strategies to relevant stakeholders, fostering a culture of transparency and accountability.

Therefore, operational risk management is not a one-time endeavor; it's an ongoing process. Regular monitoring allows organizations to adapt and enhance their risk management strategies, learning from incidents and continuously improving their operational resilience.

Also, alignment with regulatory compliance is intrinsic to operational risk management. Organizations ensure that their practices adhere to industry regulations and compliance requirements, mitigating the risk of regulatory sanctions.

Integrating operational risk management within the broader GRC framework ensures a holistic approach to governance, risk, and compliance. This alignment ensures that operational risk management is not viewed in isolation but as an integral component contributing to broader organizational objectives.

In sum, operational risk in GRC demands a proactive and comprehensive ballet. By identifying, assessing, and mitigating risks associated with people, processes, systems, and external factors, organizations fortify their operational resilience, ensuring the uninterrupted flow of essential functions and minimizing the potential financial impact of operational disruptions.

3. **Strategic Risk:**

This involves the potential negative consequences of strategic decisions, strategic risk management ensures that organizational strategies align with risk tolerance and are continually monitored for effectiveness.

In the vast landscape of Governance, Risk, and Compliance (GRC), strategic risk emerges as a dynamic force, embodying the potential for adverse outcomes stemming from the intricate realm of strategic decision-making. Unlike the tangible risks associated with operations or finances, strategic risk is intertwined with the pivotal choices made at the upper echelons of an organization, bearing the weight of uncertainties, market shifts, and the intricacies of a global business stage.

If you are trying to create a mental picture, you can imagine strategic risk as the silent undercurrent beneath decisions that shape an organization's trajectory. From entering new markets to developing products or engaging in mergers and acquisitions, strategic initiatives can either propel an organization forward or expose it to unforeseen challenges. The ebb and flow of market dynamics, external influences like technological advances or geopolitical events, all contribute to the tapestry of strategic risk, urging organizations to navigate with both caution and foresight.

Mitigating strategic risk involves a delicate dance of scenario planning and analysis, where organizations proactively envision potential futures, allowing them to make decisions aligned with a spectrum of potential outcomes. The ability to innovate and adapt is a beacon in this landscape, guiding organizations to not only weather uncertainties but to thrive in an ever-changing environment.

The competitive landscape forms a battleground for strategic risk, where organizations must not only define their strategies but also remain vigilant to the moves of competitors. Long-term planning emerges as a strategic shield, enabling organizations to identify risks and craft strategies that balance short-term gains with enduring sustainability.

Flexibility in execution is the heartbeat of strategic risk management. The capacity to adjust plans based on real-time feedback and evolving circumstances is paramount. Communication becomes the symphony, resonating transparency in strategic decisions, potential risks, and mitigation strategies, fostering stakeholder confidence and engagement.

Integrating strategic risk within the broader GRC framework is akin to weaving a tapestry where risk management aligns seamlessly with overarching governance objectives. This integration ensures a holistic approach, where strategic risk becomes an integral part of the organization's DNA, identified, assessed, and managed in harmony with other governance facets.

What strategic risk does in sum is that it beckons a mindset of foresight and adaptability. By recognizing the uncertainties inherent in strategic decisions, organizations can proactively navigate the complexities, implementing measures to identify, assess, and manage strategic risks. In this way, they not only safeguard their long-term objectives but also emerge resilient in the face of a dynamic and ever-evolving business environment.

4. **Compliance Risk:**

This pertains to the potential failure to adhere to laws, regulations, and internal policies, compliance risk management involves tracking regulatory changes, ensuring ongoing compliance, and implementing controls to mitigate non-compliance risks.

Compliance risk, within the intricate tapestry of Governance, Risk, and Compliance (GRC), unfolds as a critical realm where the potential for adverse consequences looms over organizations that falter in adhering to laws, regulations, industry standards, and internal policies. This facet is akin to a navigational challenge, demanding organizations to traverse the complex landscape of ever-changing legal requirements while safeguarding their reputation and legal standing.

You can imagine compliance risk as a dynamic terrain, intricately linked to the regulatory environment in which organizations operate. The failure to align with applicable laws and regulations can lead to not just legal repercussions but also financial penalties and reputational harm, highlighting the multifaceted nature of compliance risk.

In this dynamic landscape, compliance risk is not static; it evolves with changes in laws, industry standards, and external expectations. Organizations face the perpetual challenge of staying informed and adapting their practices to align with these evolving compliance requirements, ensuring resilience against potential risks.

Each industry comes with its unique set of compliance demands, adding layers of complexity to the risk landscape. Organizations must tailor their compliance strategies, recognizing and navigating the nuances in regulations specific to their industry.

Within the organizational realm, compliance risk extends beyond external regulations to internal policies and procedures. Ensuring internal policies align seamlessly with external regulations becomes paramount, as any inconsistencies can open the door to compliance breaches and associated risks.

A crucial aspect of managing compliance risk lies in meticulous documentation and record-keeping. Organizations must maintain accurate and comprehensive records of their compliance efforts, not just as a means of accountability but also as evidence in case of audits.

Non-compliance, beyond legal consequences, introduces a spectrum of risks including reputational damage, loss of customer trust, and strained stakeholder relationships. Hence, establishing robust compliance frameworks becomes a strategic imperative. These frameworks encompass policies, procedures, monitoring mechanisms, and training programs to ensure a comprehensive and proactive approach to compliance risk management.

For compliance, training and awareness emerge as powerful tools. Regular programs ensure that employees are well-versed in compliance requirements, fostering a culture where every member of the workforce understands their role in maintaining a compliant environment.

Given the expanding complexity of compliance landscapes, technology becomes a key ally. Automated compliance management systems can streamline processes, track changes in regulations, and facilitate timely adherence, presenting organizations with a technological advantage in managing compliance risk.

Third-party relationships introduce another layer of complexity to compliance risk. Organizations must assess and manage compliance risks associated with vendors, partners, and other third parties to mitigate potential vulnerabilities and ensure a comprehensive risk management approach.

Also, proactive monitoring and auditing form integral components of effective compliance risk management. Regular audits, internal reviews, and monitoring mechanisms help identify and address compliance issues before they escalate, instilling a proactive stance in risk mitigation.

Communication and transparency become critical elements in managing compliance risk. Transparent reporting on compliance efforts not only demonstrates the organization's commitment to adherence but also builds trust among stakeholders, positioning the organization as a responsible corporate entity.

Embracing a culture of continuous improvement ensures that compliance strategies evolve with changing regulatory landscapes and industry dynamics. In essence, compliance risk management is not a one-time endeavor; it's an ongoing process that demands diligence, adaptability, and a commitment to upholding the highest standards of legal and ethical conduct.

5. **Reputational Risk:**

It involves potential harm to an organization's reputation, reputational risk management focuses on fostering a positive corporate culture, crisis management planning, and addressing issues that could harm the organization's image.

The GRC approach to risk management is systematic, involving stages such as risk identification, assessment, mitigation, and continuous monitoring:

Reputational risk unfurls as a complex landscape where the peril of harm to an organization's image and standing with stakeholders takes center stage. This multifaceted facet is woven from various threads, including operational stumbles, ethical lapses, compliance lapses, and crises, requiring vigilant management as an organization's reputation is often its most prized asset.

To use an art allusion, you can imagine reputational risk as a delicate dance, where missteps in operations or ethical conduct can tarnish an organization's image, impacting brand perception, customer loyalty, and overall trust in the market. Non-compliance with laws and regulations becomes another thread in this tapestry, potentially leading to legal issues, regulatory fines, and a loss of stakeholder confidence.

Crisis situations serve as amplifiers, intensifying reputational risk. Effective crisis management, marked by transparent communication and swift resolution, becomes crucial in mitigating potential damage during challenging times. The rise of social media adds a new dimension, accelerating the spread of information—both positive and negative—requiring organizations to actively manage their online presence and respond promptly to mitigate potential reputational harm.

Reputational risk is closely intertwined with customer perception, as dissatisfaction, especially when amplified through social media or other channels, can quickly escalate challenges. Investors, too, closely monitor an organization's reputation, and any damage can lead to reduced confidence, impacting stock prices and overall financial health.

Building and maintaining trust are foundational to weathering reputational risk. Customer trust is the culmination of efforts that go above and beyond the development of a security posture (Neuwirth 2023). Stakeholder relationships, encompassing customers, employees, investors, and the broader community, require active management to mitigate reputational challenges. Proactive communication, especially during challenging times, becomes a strategic imperative to shape the narrative and demonstrate commitment to addressing issues.

Monitoring is crucial for early detection of reputational risks. Early warning systems and continuous monitoring allow organizations to identify potential issues and take preventive measures before they escalate. Engaging in socially responsible practices through Corporate Social Responsibility (CSR) efforts contributes to reputational resilience, building a positive image.

Conducting a reputational risk assessment is a proactive measure where organizations assess potential risks, vulnerabilities, and areas of improvement to enhance their ability to manage reputational challenges. Employee behavior also plays a pivotal role, influencing reputation. Organizations must foster a culture of ethical conduct, ensuring that employees understand their role in preserving the organization's reputation.

In short, reputational risk in GRC demands a delicate balance and proactive engagement. By addressing potential issues proactively, transparently communicating during crises, and actively managing relationships with stakeholders, organizations can navigate the complex landscape of reputational risk, upholding the trust and confidence of their stakeholders.

6. **Risk Identification:**

Risk identification involves a comprehensive assessment of internal and external factors, historical data, and industry trends to identify potential risks.

It can be compared to an intricate exploration, where organizations systematically uncover and comprehend potential risks that could impact their objectives. This proactive journey involves several strategic steps and considerations to ensure a comprehensive understanding and effective management of risks.

In the initial stages, engaging with stakeholders becomes a foundational step. By seeking input from diverse perspectives such as employees, management, customers, and regulatory bodies, organizations gain valuable insights into a spectrum of potential risks. This collaborative approach sets the stage for a more holistic risk identification process.

Categorizing risks into various types, such as strategic, operational, financial, compliance, and reputational, allows organizations to encompass a wide array of potential challenges. This comprehensive categorization ensures that no critical risk aspect is overlooked, fostering a robust risk management strategy.

Analyzing historical data and trends becomes a guidepost in this exploration. By reviewing past incidents and trends, organizations can glean insights into recurring risks, allowing for a more informed and anticipatory risk management approach. Additionally, scenario planning, involving the creation of hypothetical situations, aids in identifying potential future risks and fortifying organizational preparedness.

The legal and regulatory landscape is a key terrain to traverse in risk identification. Non-compliance poses inherent risks, and a thorough understanding of the legal and regulatory environment ensures that compliance risks are recognized and effectively addressed.

The evolving technological landscape introduces its own set of risks. Organizations must assess the risks related to cybersecurity, data breaches, and technology failures in today's digital era, ensuring that they stay ahead of potential technological challenges.

External factors, ranging from economic conditions to geopolitical events and market trends, form an external environmental analysis that impacts organizational risk. Recognizing these external risks, even beyond the organization's control, is crucial for effective risk management.

An inward gaze at internal processes helps identify operational risks. By evaluating the efficiency and effectiveness of internal processes, organizations can pinpoint areas susceptible to risks and implement measures for improvement.

Collaborative sessions, such as risk workshops and brainstorming, harness the collective intelligence of key stakeholders. These sessions uncover risks that may not be apparent through other methods, fostering a culture of shared risk awareness.

Also, Key Performance Indicators (KPIs) serve as vital signposts in the risk identification journey. Monitoring KPIs aids in early risk detection, allowing organizations to align risk identification with performance metrics and respond promptly to deviations.

Another way to facilitate real-time risk monitoring is to leverage technology and analytics. Utilizing risk management software and analytics tools empowers organizations to identify and respond to risks in a timely manner, aligning with the dynamic nature of risk landscapes.

Maintaining a risk register acts as a central repository for identified risks, documenting their likelihood, impact, and mitigation strategies. This documentation provides a comprehensive overview that guides ongoing risk management efforts.

Continuous monitoring, coupled with feedback mechanisms that encourage employees to report potential risks, ensures that the organization remains vigilant and adaptable to evolving risks and changing business environments.

To cap, risk identification in GRC unfolds as a dynamic, collaborative, and forward-thinking exploration, where organizations navigate various terrains to uncover potential risks comprehensively. This process lays the foundation for a robust risk management strategy that enables organizations to proactively address challenges and safeguard their objectives.

7. **Risk Assessment:**

Risk assessment evaluates the likelihood and impact of identified risks to prioritize them and determine the level of attention and resources required. Risk management failures at major corporations have captured the headlines for many years, primarily in the financial sector, but in other sectors as well, and have not always been the result of shortcomings in financial risk-taking (OECD 2014).

Embarking on the journey of risk assessment within the domain of Governance, Risk, and Compliance (GRC) is akin to a meticulous expedition where organizations systematically scrutinize potential risks. This structured process unfolds through various stages, each contributing to a comprehensive understanding of the risks at hand and informing strategies for their effective management.

The initiation point is the identification of risks, a process that can be approached through diverse methods such as stakeholder engagement, historical data analysis, scenario planning, and specialized assessments, especially in the technological domain. Once risks are identified, categorization becomes a strategic move, grouping them into classifications like financial, operational, strategic, compliance, and reputational. This categorization sets the stage for a more focused and nuanced assessment.

Understanding the potential impact of each risk is paramount. Organizations delve into impact analysis, evaluating the consequences a risk may pose across different facets, including financial stability, operational efficiency, reputation, and compliance standing. Concurrently, assessing the likelihood of a risk materializing adds a crucial dimension to the evaluation process. Organizations consider historical data, industry trends, and external factors to gauge the probability of each identified risk coming to fruition.

The culmination of impact and likelihood assessments results in risk scoring, a numeric representation that aids in prioritization. High scores signal risks that demand immediate attention and resource allocation. Simultaneously, the evaluation of existing controls forms a critical step, where organizations scrutinize the effectiveness of current risk mitigation measures, including internal controls and compliance protocols.

Aligning risk assessment with organizational risk appetite and tolerance levels is integral. By defining these thresholds, organizations ensure that the risk assessment process resonates with their strategic objectives and the level of risk they are willing to bear. Documentation and reporting play a key role in maintaining transparency. Comprehensive documentation includes details on identified risks, assessment criteria, scores, and recommended mitigation strategies. Reporting to stakeholders ensures that decision-makers are well-informed. It is important to note that effective risk management is not about eliminating risk taking, which is indeed a fundamental driving force in business and entrepreneurship (OECD 2014).

The outcome of risk assessment is not merely identification; it extends to the formulation of mitigation strategies. Organizations develop and prioritize strategies to mitigate identified risks, considering factors such as cost-effectiveness and feasibility. This involves implementing new controls or strengthening existing ones to fortify the organization's resilience.

Risk assessment is not a one-time endeavor but an ongoing process, seamlessly integrated with continuous monitoring. This adaptive approach ensures that organizations remain responsive to evolving risks, enabling regular reassessment and adjustment of risk management strategies based on changes in the business environment.

Further enriching the risk assessment process is scenario analysis, where organizations simulate hypothetical situations to understand potential cascading effects of risks. This enhances their preparedness for complex and dynamic challenges. Training and awareness initiatives are integral to building a risk-aware culture among employees, fostering a proactive approach to risk management.

In simple but vivid terms, you could summarise risk assessment in GRC to be a strategic and dynamic voyage, involving meticulous analysis, thoughtful categorization, and proactive mitigation. By navigating through these stages, organizations fortify themselves against potential challenges, creating a resilient foundation for sustained success in an ever-evolving business landscape.

8. Risk Mitigation:

Encompasses the implementation of strategies and controls to reduce the likelihood and impact of risks or devising contingency plans to manage them effectively.

Risk mitigation then becomes a strategic process aimed at fortifying organizations against potential threats. It's a proactive journey, employing a spectrum of measures to curtail the impact and likelihood of identified risks, safeguarding an organization's objectives, assets, and reputation.

One cornerstone of risk mitigation involves the implementation of preventive controls. Organizations bolster their defenses by fortifying cybersecurity protocols, conducting thorough due diligence before entering partnerships, and establishing robust internal controls, aiming to prevent risks from materializing in the first place. Simultaneously, having corrective actions in place is crucial. Incident response plans, crisis communication strategies, and contingency plans become the toolkit for addressing risks swiftly and effectively when they inevitably occur (Appazov, 2014).

Diversification of assets stands out as another mitigation strategy, where resources are spread strategically to minimize the impact of a single risk. This could involve diversifying investment portfolios, maintaining multiple suppliers, and ensuring a diversified customer base. Insurance coverage is leveraged to transfer financial risk, with organizations procuring insurance policies tailored to cover various risks such as property damage, liability, and business interruption.

Similarly, contractual agreements play a pivotal role in risk mitigation, as organizations use legal mechanisms to allocate responsibilities and liabilities effectively. Clarity in contracts, including indemnification clauses, serves as a risk mitigation strategy. Training and awareness programs emerge as integral components, equipping employees with the knowledge and understanding needed to identify and mitigate risks. Regular training on compliance, cybersecurity best practices, and ethical conduct fosters a culture of risk awareness.

Continuous monitoring becomes a vigilant practice, with organizations utilizing monitoring tools for cybersecurity threats, regularly reviewing financial transactions for anomalies, and staying informed about regulatory changes. Regular audits and assessments are conducted to periodically evaluate the effectiveness of risk mitigation measures, ensuring ongoing resilience. Stakeholder communication is prioritized during crises, with organizations establishing communication plans to keep stakeholders informed and maintaining transparent dialogue with regulators.

Therefore, cross-functional collaboration becomes imperative, fostering teamwork among different departments to comprehensively address risks. Regulatory compliance is prioritized, with organizations regularly reviewing and updating policies and procedures to stay aligned with changing regulations. Scenario planning, involving the anticipation and planning for potential scenarios, becomes a strategic practice, and strategic risk management integrates risk considerations into the core of strategic planning.

Investment in technology emerges as a modern approach to risk mitigation, with organizations leveraging advanced tools for cybersecurity, utilizing data analytics for risk prediction, and adopting GRC software for streamlined management.

9. **Continuous Monitoring:**

This involves regular monitoring of the risk landscape to identify emerging risks, reassess existing ones, and adapt risk management strategies accordingly.

Continuous monitoring unfolds as a vigilant and ongoing process, akin to a watchful guardian ensuring the resilience and integrity of an organization. In this dynamic approach, real-time risk identification takes center stage, employing advanced monitoring tools and technologies to promptly detect anomalies, security threats, and deviations from established norms.

Ensuring ongoing compliance with regulatory requirements becomes a fundamental pillar of continuous monitoring. Automated systems track changes in regulations, assess their implications on the organization, and swiftly implement necessary compliance measures, maintaining a proactive stance in the face of evolving regulatory landscapes.

The continuous assessment of key performance indicators (KPIs) stands as a crucial aspect, allowing organizations to regularly monitor and analyze these metrics. This ongoing scrutiny provides insights into trends, deviations, and areas requiring improvement, facilitating agile decision-making and prompt corrective actions.

In the realm of cybersecurity, continuous monitoring involves the surveillance of the organization's digital landscape. Leveraging cybersecurity tools and technologies, entities actively detect and respond to potential security incidents, safeguarding sensitive data and maintaining the integrity of digital assets.

Data integrity assurance is another facet of continuous monitoring, where organizations implement processes and checks to ensure the accuracy and consistency of organizational data. This includes validation procedures to identify and rectify any discrepancies promptly, upholding the reliability of critical information.

Monitoring adherence to established policies and procedures is paramount. Regular reviews assess whether employees and processes align with established guidelines, allowing organizations to take corrective action in case of any deviations and ensuring consistency in operational practices.

Vendor risk management is integrated into the continuous monitoring process, involving regular assessments of the security posture of third-party vendors. Organizations ensure that vendors comply with security and privacy standards, promptly addressing any identified risks associated with external partnerships.

Incident response readiness is upheld through continuous testing and updating of incident response plans. Simulations and ongoing training programs ensure that personnel are well-prepared to respond effectively to various types of incidents, minimizing/ potential damages.

The application of data analytics to identify patterns and trends becomes a strategic component of continuous monitoring. Utilizing data analysis tools, organizations gain insights into trends, anomalies, and potential risks, enabling informed decision-making and proactive risk management.

Continuous employee training and awareness initiatives form an integral part of the process, ensuring that employees are consistently educated about risks and compliance requirements. Regular training sessions and awareness programs keep the workforce informed about the latest developments, fostering a culture of vigilance and responsibility.

Environmental scanning, encompassing the monitoring of external factors impacting the business environment, remains an ongoing practice. Staying informed about industry trends, geopolitical developments, and other external factors allows organizations to adapt strategies promptly to mitigate risks or capitalize on emerging opportunities.

Establishing feedback loops completes the cycle of continuous monitoring. Encouraging employees to provide feedback on GRC processes creates channels for continuous improvement, ensuring that the organization remains adaptive and responsive to changing circumstances.

So, continuous monitoring in GRC embodies a proactive, adaptive, and multifaceted approach. Leveraging technology, data analytics, and a commitment to ongoing improvement, organizations can navigate the dynamic landscape of risks and compliance, fortifying their resilience and ensuring the sustained success of their operations.

To wrap up the breakdown of risk, when viewed through the lens of GRC, is not solely considered a threat; it is also recognized as an opportunity for growth and innovation. By adopting a proactive approach to risk management, organizations can enhance their resilience, make informed decisions, and create a culture that embraces calculated risk-taking within acceptable parameters. Managing risk effectively is a dynamic and ongoing process that is fundamental to the success and sustainability of an organization in the complex and ever-evolving business landscape.

1.3 DECIPHERING COMPLIANCE

Simply put, compliance focuses on adhering to laws, regulations, industry standards, and internal policies. It ensures that an organization operates within legal and ethical boundaries, mitigating the risk of legal issues, reputational damage, and financial losses.

Compliance within the realm of Governance, Risk, and Compliance (GRC) is the bedrock of an organization's commitment to operating within established legal, regulatory, and ethical frameworks. It encompasses a multifaceted set of practices and processes aimed at ensuring that the actions and operations of an organization align with external laws, regulations, industry standards, and internal policies.

Legal compliance involves adhering to the extensive array of laws and regulations that govern the organization's operations, encompassing local, national, and international levels. Regulatory compliance extends this commitment to industry-specific regulations relevant to the organization's sector.

Internally, compliance is about ensuring alignment with the organization's own policies and procedures. These internal guidelines reflect the organization's values, ethical standards, and operational requirements. It involves more than just ticking boxes; it necessitates a cultural integration where every member of the organization understands and embraces their role in maintaining compliance.

Compliance efforts are not static; they demand constant monitoring, assessment, and adjustment to changes in laws, regulations, and industry standards. Regular audits and assessments are integral components of compliance strategies, ensuring ongoing adherence and identifying areas for improvement.

Training and awareness initiatives play a crucial role in fostering a culture of compliance. By investing in programs that educate employees about compliance requirements, organizations empower individuals at all levels to contribute to a culture of responsibility and accountability.

The consequences of non-compliance can be severe, ranging from legal penalties and financial losses to reputational harm. Hence, GRC strategies prioritize preventing non-compliance and responding swiftly to any breaches that may occur.

So you could in essence say that compliance in GRC is a dynamic and comprehensive approach that extends beyond the realm of legal adherence. It is about embodying a commitment to ethical conduct, internal policies, and external regulations. By integrating compliance seamlessly into the broader GRC framework, organizations not only meet legal obligations but also build trust, enhance their reputation, and contribute to their long-term sustainability and success.

1.4 The Interconnected Nature of GRC

The interconnected nature of Governance, Risk, and Compliance (GRC) is akin to the intricate threads that weave through the fabric of organizational management, forming a comprehensive and interdependent framework. This interconnectedness reflects the symbiotic relationship among these three components, illustrating how governance sets the stage for risk management and compliance efforts, and how effective integration of these elements contributes to organizational success.

1.4.1 Governance as the Foundation

As has been explained earlier, governance is at the heart of this interconnected triad, as it serves as the foundational structure that dictates how an organization operates. Governance establishes the rules, processes, and decision-making frameworks that guide the behavior of individuals within the organization. It defines roles, responsibilities, and the overarching mission, aligning the organization's actions with its strategic objectives and ethical standards.

At its core, governance is the compass that guides the organization's strategic direction, outlining the mission, vision, and values that underpin decision-making. This strategic alignment is the linchpin that harmonizes risk management and compliance endeavors with the overarching organizational strategy. Governance ensures that efforts to mitigate risks and meet compliance standards are seamlessly integrated into the fabric of the organization's broader goals.

Risk oversight, another vital dimension of GRC, is entrusted to governance structures such as boards and executive leadership. These entities not only set the risk appetite but also provide vigilant oversight, steering the organization away from potential pitfalls. This interconnected nature ensures that risk management becomes an integral part of everyday operations, fostering a culture where risks are identified, assessed, and addressed in alignment with the organization's risk tolerance.

The compliance framework, deeply rooted in governance principles, serves as a guidepost for ethical standards and regulatory adherence. Governance establishes policies and procedures that define the boundaries within which the organization must operate. This interconnectedness ensures that compliance with laws and regulations is not a separate function but an inherent aspect of the organization's operational DNA.

Decision-making processes, orchestrated by governance structures, reflect the interconnected nature of GRC. Boards and executives, in their strategic decisions, conscientiously consider both risks and compliance obligations. Governance ensures that decisions are made with a holistic understanding, incorporating risk assessments and compliance implications, thereby contributing to a well-informed and balanced approach.

Accountability and transparency, fostered by governance, further solidify the interconnectedness of GRC. Governance defines roles, responsibilities, and reporting structures, instilling a culture of accountability. This culture is integral to GRC, ensuring that individuals and departments are held responsible for managing risks and complying with standards. Transparency is achieved through clear reporting on risk exposure and compliance status, reinforcing the symbiotic relationship between these elements.

Continuous improvement, encouraged by governance, forms the capstone of the interconnected nature of GRC. Governance sets expectations for performance and outcomes, providing the framework for evaluating and enhancing organizational processes. This culture of continuous improvement in GRC involves learning from experiences, adapting strategies, and evolving risk management and compliance practices in response to changing landscapes.

1.4.2. Risk Management as a Strategic Navigator

Building upon the foundation of governance, risk management emerges as a strategic navigator within the GRC framework. Governance structures set the parameters for risk-taking, and risk management, in turn, involves the identification, assessment, and mitigation of uncertainties that could impact the achievement of organizational goals. It is a dynamic process that necessitates a thorough understanding of an organization's risk appetite and tolerance.

In other words, this strategic navigator becomes an essential tool for steering the course of the organization towards its objectives while adeptly navigating potential risks.

In the role of setting the course, risk management proactively charts the organization's path by identifying and understanding potential risks that could impede progress. This strategic foresight transforms risk management into a proactive guide, empowering decision-makers with insights crucial for informed decision-making and strategic planning.

Aligning with organizational objectives, risk management ceases to exist as a detached function and seamlessly integrates into the strategic fabric of the organization. This alignment ensures that efforts to mitigate risks are not at odds with strategic goals but rather contribute to the overarching mission.

As a compass in navigating uncertainty, risk management equips organizations with the tools and methodologies to assess and navigate unpredictable market changes, regulatory shifts, and unforeseen events. This adaptability is paramount for maintaining resilience and agility in the face of ever-evolving business landscapes.

Fostering innovation becomes a hallmark of risk management as a strategic navigator. By encouraging a proactive approach to risk, organizations can embrace calculated risks that propel innovation and growth. This delicate balance between risk-taking and risk mitigation creates a dynamic environment conducive to strategic advancements.

Safeguarding reputation is an integral facet of risk management's strategic navigation. It guides the implementation of measures to protect against reputational risks, ensuring that decisions align with ethical standards and stakeholder expectations. In doing so, risk management becomes a guardian of the organization's credibility.

Adapting to change is a crucial function of risk management as a strategic navigator. It equips organizations with the ability to respond proactively to evolving circumstances, be it internal changes or external influences. This strategic adaptability ensures that organizations can navigate shifts in the regulatory landscape, technological advancements, and market dynamics.

Continuous improvement is woven into the fabric of risk management's strategic navigation. Through ongoing monitoring, assessment, and refinement of risk management strategies, organizations learn from experiences and enhance their ability to navigate future challenges. This iterative process transforms risk management into a dynamic and evolving strategic navigator, ensuring its relevance in the ever-changing landscape of GRC.

1.4.3. Compliance as the Safeguard

Within the intricate interplay of Governance, Risk, and Compliance (GRC), compliance takes on the role of a vigilant safeguard, a steadfast bulwark against potential challenges. Far beyond a mere checklist, Compliance, in its capacity as the safeguard, becomes an integral force in organizational governance, contributing to stability, integrity, and sustained success.

As the sentinel of ethical conduct, Compliance stands as a vigilant guardian, ensuring that every facet of organizational behavior aligns with unwavering ethical standards. In upholding these principles, Compliance becomes not only a protector of the organization's reputation but a curator of a culture rooted in integrity and trust.

Functioning as a shield against legal risks, Compliance acts as a guardian, meticulously guiding the organization to adhere to applicable laws and regulations. This proactive stance serves as a shield, mitigating the risk of legal liabilities, lawsuits, and regulatory sanctions. By navigating the legal landscape with precision, Compliance minimizes uncertainties, contributing to the organization's overarching risk management strategy.

Upholding regulatory standards becomes a defining attribute of Compliance in its safeguard role. It ensures that the organization operates within the defined parameters set by regulatory bodies, minimizing the risk of non-compliance penalties and establishing a cooperative relationship with regulatory authorities.

Integration into business processes is a hallmark of Compliance as the safeguard. Rather than existing as a detached entity, Compliance seamlessly integrates into day-to-day operations. This ensures that compliance considerations are intrinsic to decision-making processes, reducing the risk of unintentional non-compliance.

Compliance, as a risk mitigator, establishes and enforces robust policies and procedures. This structured framework guides employees in adhering to regulatory requirements and ethical standards. By setting clear guidelines, Compliance contributes to risk mitigation and ensures a consistent approach to compliance across the organization.

Functioning as a cultural beacon, Compliance shapes the ethos of the organization. It fosters a culture where compliance is not perceived as a burdensome obligation but as a shared responsibility. This cultural alignment ensures that every member of the organization becomes an active participant in safeguarding compliance standards.

The role of compliance as the safeguard extends to continuous monitoring and adaptation. Beyond static adherence, Compliance embraces a dynamic approach, allowing for the timely identification of emerging compliance challenges. This agility enables the organization to adapt swiftly to evolving regulatory landscapes, reinforcing its resilience.

1.5 The Continuous Loop of Interdependence

The interconnected nature of GRC is not a linear progression; rather, it is a continuous loop of interdependence. Governance structures influence risk management strategies, which, in turn, inform compliance measures. Compliance activities feed back into governance by providing insights for continuous improvement. This iterative process reflects the adaptability and responsiveness required in the ever-evolving landscape of business, regulations, and risks.

That is, each element plays a vital role in sustaining organizational integrity and effectiveness in the continuous loop of interdependence which is a dynamic and interconnected cycle. It establishes the framework of policies and decision-making structures, setting the stage for the interdependence that follows.

Risk steps into the narrative as the catalyst, introducing an element of unpredictability and opportunity. It injects dynamism into the loop, prompting organizations to assess potential challenges and opportunities. Risk management becomes the means by which organizations navigate uncertainties, making informed decisions that align with governance structures and compliance standards.

Compliance takes on the role of the sentinel, standing guard to ensure adherence to established norms. It acts as the vigilant protector of governance principles, ensuring that policies and procedures are not only created but consistently followed. Compliance reinforces the loop by providing a set of standards against which governance decisions and risk management strategies are evaluated.

In this symphony of interdependence, governance, risk, and compliance harmonize, creating a resilient and adaptable organizational framework. The loop relies on the orchestration of these elements in unison. Governance informs risk and compliance strategies, risk management adapts to compliance requirements, and compliance ensures that governance principles are upheld.

Feedback emerges as the refining agent, providing insights for continuous improvement. The loop thrives on feedback mechanisms that allow for ongoing refinement. Insights from compliance audits, risk assessments, and governance evaluations feed back into the loop, influencing future decisions and strategies. This iterative process ensures adaptability and responsiveness.

Organizational learning becomes the growth spurt in this narrative, fostering adaptability and innovation. The loop's vitality relies on the organization's ability to learn from experiences. Through continuous learning, organizations evolve, developing the capacity to navigate new challenges and seize emerging opportunities.

At the core of this narrative is adaptability, the fundamental tenet that allows the loop to flex and adjust to changing circumstances. The continuous loop thrives on its ability to adapt, facing shifting regulatory landscapes, emerging risks, or evolving governance frameworks. This adaptability ensures that the interdependence remains robust and relevant over time.

1.6 Technology and Data Integration

In the modern business landscape, technology plays a pivotal role in facilitating the interconnected nature of GRC. Integrated GRC platforms leverage technology to streamline processes, automate data collection and analysis, and provide real-time insights. This integration enhances the organization's ability to make informed decisions, manage risks effectively, and ensure compliance with changing regulatory landscapes.

In this regard, technology assumes the role of a catalyst, propelling GRC into a new era of efficiency and sophistication. It transcends its conventional role as a tool and transforms into an enabler, fostering streamlined governance structures, intricate risk management strategies, and precise compliance efforts. The synergy of technology intricately weaves into the GRC fabric, optimizing processes, and unlocking new dimensions of organizational effectiveness.

Data, in this narrative, emerges as the strategic nexus, the lifeblood that fuels informed decision-making. It transcends its status as mere information and becomes a valuable asset, offering insights that shape governance frameworks, inform risk assessments, and ensure compliance with ever-evolving standards. The strategic utilization of data transforms information into actionable intelligence, fortifying the very core of the GRC ecosystem.

Integration becomes the seamless tapestry weaving technology and data into the GRC framework. It goes beyond breaking down isolated applications, fostering a holistic environment where data flows seamlessly across governance, risk, and compliance functions. This integration eradicates silos, offering a unified view of organizational activities and empowering more effective decision-making.

Automation emerges as the efficiency engine in this narrative, streamlining routine tasks and augmenting human capabilities. It liberates resources from mundane processes, allowing personnel to focus on strategic initiatives. Automated risk assessments, compliance tracking, and real-time data analytics become the driving force, enhancing the agility and responsiveness of the GRC ecosystem.

Then, predictive analytics assumes the role of the foresight tool, transcending historical data to provide a forward-looking perspective. It aids in proactive risk management and strategic planning, transforming data into a strategic asset that equips organizations to navigate uncertainties with foresight.

Cybersecurity, in this narrative, becomes the shield safeguarding data integrity and protecting against digital threats. It stands as an integral component of the GRC narrative, ensuring that technology and data integration occur within a secure and resilient environment. Cybersecurity measures become a proactive force, fortifying the organization against potential risks inherent in the digital landscape.

Continuous innovation emerges as the guiding principle, acknowledging the rapid evolution of technology and data practices. It encourages organizations to embrace innovation as a constant, positioning GRC as a forward-looking discipline ready to leverage emerging technologies for sustained excellence.

You could then say that the intertwining saga of Technology and Data Integration in GRC unveils a story of strategic alignment. It involves the harmonious integration of technology as an enabler and data as a strategic asset, forming a cohesive tapestry that enhances governance structures, refines risk management strategies, and ensures compliance with precision. This narrative positions GRC as a dynamic and adaptive discipline, leveraging the power of technology and data to navigate the complexities of the modern organizational landscape.

1.7 Organizational Culture as the Glue

Beyond the formal structures, the interconnectedness of GRC is embedded in the organizational culture. A culture of responsibility, transparency, and ethical conduct is the glue that binds governance, risk management, and compliance together. It influences how employees perceive their roles in GRC and shapes their behaviors in alignment with organizational values.

It transcends the role of a mere backdrop, actively shaping how governance is enacted, risks are managed, and compliance is embraced within the organizational landscape.

Let's deploy some architectural imagery. See organizational culture as the overarching framework, a silent architect that molds the norms and values guiding GRC practices. It lays down the ethical compass by which governance decisions unfold, risk assessments take shape, and compliance standards are upheld. This cultural framework becomes the bedrock upon which the entire GRC structure is anchored.

Within this framework, organizational culture infuses values into governance, ensuring that decision-making aligns seamlessly with the organization's mission. It transforms governance into a reflection of the organization's core values, fostering an ethical decision-making process deeply rooted in the identity and purpose of the organization.

The influence of organizational culture extends to the appetite for risk-taking, delicately balancing the organization's willingness to embrace innovation and calculated risks. It becomes the guiding force that shapes the approach to risk management, establishing the equilibrium between risk aversion and a forward-looking risk acceptance that can spur innovation and resilience within the GRC framework.

In this cultural narrative, compliance evolves beyond a set of rules to become a cultural norm. Organizational Culture embeds adherence to rules and regulations into the daily fabric of operations, fostering a compliance mindset that is not just a requirement but a shared commitment woven into the very DNA of the organization.

Communication and transparency stand as fundamental pillars within the realm of Organizational Culture. The culture values open communication, ensuring that information flows seamlessly across GRC functions. Transparency becomes a norm, facilitating effective risk reporting, governance communication, and compliance monitoring.

Employee engagement takes center stage in the cultural narrative of GRC. Organizational Culture places a premium on engagement, recognizing that an involved workforce is an asset in GRC initiatives. It fosters a sense of ownership and responsibility, encouraging employees to actively participate in governance processes, contribute to risk identification, and embrace compliance standards.

Furthermore, Continual learning and adaptability become ingrained traits within the cultural landscape. Organizational Culture values the importance of evolving with the dynamic GRC landscape. It creates an environment where the organization is not just receptive but thrives on continuous learning, adjusting strategies, and remaining agile in the face of evolving governance, risk, and compliance challenges.

CHAPTER TWO

THE EVOLUTION OF GRC

The evolution of Governance, Risk, and Compliance (GRC) is a dynamic journey that has unfolded in response to the changing landscape of business, regulations, and the recognition of the interconnected nature of these critical organizational functions.

Given the dynamism of the factors and variables that inform GRC, the concept of evolution emerges as a dynamic and transformative journey, signifying the continual adaptation and growth of these critical organizational elements. An analysis of GRC's evolution is done below:

2.1 The Stages of GRC's Evolution

2.1.1 The Origins and Early Frameworks

The evolution of GRC traces back to its origins, shaped by early frameworks and foundational principles. In its nascent stages, GRC was a response to the need for cohesive structures to govern organizations, manage risks, and ensure compliance. Basic frameworks laid the groundwork for what would later become a sophisticated and integrated discipline.

2.1.2 Integration of Governance, Risk, and Compliance

GRC evolved through the integration of governance, risk management, and compliance into a unified framework. This integration marked a transformative phase, recognizing the interconnected nature of these elements. It shifted GRC from isolated practices to a holistic approach, acknowledging that effective governance requires a comprehensive understanding of both risks and compliance requirements.

2.1.3 Technological Revolution

The evolution of GRC surged forward with the advent of technology, ushering in a new era of efficiency and sophistication. Technological advancements introduced automation, data analytics, and integrated platforms, revolutionizing how organizations approach GRC. This phase empowered organizations to manage risks in real-time, streamline compliance processes, and enhance the overall effectiveness of governance structures.

2.1.4 Shift towards Proactive Risk Management

GRC evolved from reactive risk management to a more proactive approach. Organizations began to anticipate and address risks before they escalated, emphasizing strategic risk management as a key component of GRC. This shift allowed for a more agile response to emerging threats and opportunities.

2.1.5 Emphasis on Corporate Culture

The evolution of GRC included a heightened emphasis on corporate culture as a driving force. Recognizing the impact of culture on decision-making, organizations started to integrate cultural considerations into GRC frameworks. This cultural shift aimed to align governance decisions, risk management strategies, and compliance efforts with the values and mission of the organization.

2.1.6 Regulatory Landscape and Globalization

GRC evolved in response to an ever-changing regulatory landscape and increased globalization. Organizations operating across borders faced diverse regulatory requirements. GRC frameworks adapted to navigate this complexity, incorporating strategies to ensure compliance with regional and global standards while maintaining effective governance and risk management practices.

2.1.7 Continuous Learning and Adaptive Frameworks

The evolution of GRC is marked by a commitment to continuous learning and adaptive frameworks. In a rapidly changing business environment, GRC continually adapts to emerging challenges and opportunities. Organizations embrace a mindset of ongoing learning, ensuring that GRC frameworks remain agile, responsive, and relevant in the face of evolving governance, risk, and compliance landscapes.

The evolution of GRC is a dynamic journey that spans its origins to the present day, marked by key milestones such as the integration of governance, risk, and compliance, the technological revolution, a shift towards proactive risk management, a focus on corporate culture, adaptation to regulatory changes and globalization, and a commitment to continuous learning. This evolutionary narrative positions GRC as a resilient and adaptive discipline, crucial for organizations navigating the complexities of the modern business landscape.

2.2 The Business Case for GRC

Making a business case for Governance, Risk, and Compliance (GRC) is a compelling narrative and adventure that underscores the strategic advantages and intrinsic value that a robust GRC framework brings to organizations. Beyond the conventional lens of regulatory adherence, GRC emerges as a proactive and integral force shaping the trajectory of organizational success and sustainability. GRC in its cohesive nature brings about a more unified approach to solving issues that may arise in an organization.

One of the consequences of a fragmented approach to various risk management and compliance initiatives is the emergence of heterogeneous reporting structures. This prevents management from obtaining a comprehensive overview of key compliance and risk indicators, so that an integrated view of the company's compliance and risk status is not available. This is particularly important for senior management, since inadequate reporting and monitoring of GRC activities increases the risk of non-compliance.

GRC's impact on strategic decision-making is profound, laying the foundation for clear governance structures that align decisions with organizational objectives, values, and risk tolerance. This alignment fosters organizational agility and responsiveness in the face of an ever-evolving business landscape.

A cornerstone of the business case for GRC lies in its role in enhancing risk management. GRC provides organizations with the tools to identify and mitigate risks proactively, safeguarding assets, reputation, and financial stability. It becomes a strategic enabler, allowing organizations not only to navigate uncertainties but also to capitalize on emerging opportunities, ensuring long-term resilience.

Crucially, GRC addresses regulatory compliance not as an isolated function but as an integrated element of a broader framework. This ensures ethical operations and regulatory adherence, mitigating legal risks and contributing to a positive corporate image. The ethical foundation established by GRC serves as a key pillar for reputation and trust building, fostering positive relationships with stakeholders, including customers, investors, and partners.

Efficient GRC practices streamline operations, reduce redundancies, and optimize resource allocation, leading to operational efficiency and cost savings. GRC becomes a catalyst for resource optimization, focusing efforts on areas with the highest impact on organizational goals.

As stakeholder expectations evolve to value ethical conduct and responsible business practices, GRC becomes a means of aligning organizational activities with these expectations. Demonstrating a commitment to GRC principles not only enhances relationships with stakeholders but also aligns the organization with broader societal expectations.

GRC's contribution extends to crisis preparedness and resilience. Organizations with robust GRC frameworks are better equipped to face crises by establishing contingency plans and response mechanisms, ensuring a more swift recovery from challenges.

Embedded in the DNA of an organization, GRC fosters a culture of continuous improvement. It positions organizations to stay ahead of regulatory changes, emerging risks, and industry trends, showcasing adaptability in the face of a dynamic business environment.

In the global business landscape, organizations with effective GRC frameworks gain a competitive advantage. The ability to demonstrate ethical conduct, manage risks proactively, and ensure compliance differentiates organizations, contributing to market positioning and long-term success.

2.3 GRC Technologies

GRC technologies, encompassing Governance, Risk, and Compliance, have become pivotal in the modern business landscape, providing organizations with tools to navigate complexities, enhance decision-making, and ensure regulatory adherence. These technologies are designed to streamline and automate processes, offering a comprehensive approach to managing the interconnected aspects of governance, risk, and compliance. Appropriate use of technology helps companies face these challenges and increase the effectiveness and efficiency of processes required to solve them (PWC 2005).

At the core of GRC technologies is the integration of diverse functionalities into unified platforms. These platforms often include modules or features addressing governance structures, risk assessment and management, and compliance tracking. By centralizing these functions, GRC technologies facilitate a holistic view of an organization's operational landscape.

Governance aspects within GRC technologies involve the creation and maintenance of organizational structures, defining roles, responsibilities, and decision-making processes. This functionality ensures transparency and accountability, aligning organizational activities with strategic objectives.

Risk management features enable organizations to identify, assess, and mitigate potential risks. GRC technologies provide tools for scenario analysis, risk quantification, and monitoring, allowing proactive management of uncertainties that could impact organizational goals.

Compliance modules are designed to track adherence to laws, regulations, and internal policies. GRC technologies automate compliance assessments, monitor regulatory changes, and provide mechanisms for documenting and demonstrating adherence, reducing the burden of manual compliance efforts.

Integration with data analytics is a key feature of advanced GRC technologies. By leveraging data, organizations can gain insights into patterns, trends, and potential risks, enhancing the decision-making process and allowing for a more proactive approach to risk management.

The role of automation in GRC technologies is crucial for efficiency. Automated workflows, alerts, and reporting mechanisms streamline processes, reducing the likelihood of errors and ensuring that organizations can respond swiftly to emerging risks or compliance issues.

Cloud-based GRC solutions have gained prominence, offering flexibility and accessibility. These platforms allow organizations to manage GRC processes remotely, promoting collaboration among teams, and ensuring real-time updates and monitoring.

Mobile capabilities further enhance accessibility, enabling stakeholders to engage with GRC processes from anywhere, at any time. This flexibility is particularly valuable for organizations with geographically dispersed teams or those requiring quick responses to emerging issues.

As the regulatory landscape evolves, GRC technologies play a vital role in keeping organizations up-to-date. These solutions often include features for tracking regulatory changes, ensuring that compliance measures are adjusted promptly to reflect new requirements.

Therefore, GRC technologies represent a dynamic and adaptive solution for organizations seeking to manage governance, risk, and compliance effectively. By integrating diverse functionalities into cohesive platforms, these technologies empower organizations to proactively address challenges, make informed decisions, and cultivate a culture of transparency and accountability.

CHAPTER THREE

PROFESSIONALS WHO CAN VENTURE INTO GRC

Although people with tech skills relatively find the field of GRC easy to venture into, people with non-tech skills have often wondered if GRC, despite being a multifaceted field, was meant for them. It is important to know and note that GRC is a multifaceted field that welcomes professionals from various backgrounds, tech or not. Individuals with diverse skills, educational qualifications, and experiences can find fulfilling careers in GRC.The overarching goal of a GRC professional is to help organizations manage risk, ensure compliance, and promote good governance and ethical behavior(Anwari 2023)

To this end, a breakdown of people who can successfully venture into GRC is done:

3.1 WORKERS WHO CAN TRANSITION INTO GRC

I. **Risk Management Professionals**

Individuals with a background in risk management, including risk analysts, risk managers, and those with experience in identifying, assessing, and mitigating risks.

Risk management professionals form a diverse and essential cohort within organizations, specializing in the intricate art of identifying, assessing, and mitigating risks. At the forefront of this field are Risk Managers, charged with the comprehensive oversight of an organization's risk landscape. They delve into the intricacies of risk identification, develop strategies for mitigation, and align the organization's risk profile with its overarching objectives.

Chief Risk Officers (CRO) ascend to the executive level, steering the ship of overall risk management strategy. Their role involves close collaboration with senior leadership, ensuring that risk management practices seamlessly integrate with the organization's broader business goals. In the analytical realm, Risk Analysts crunch numbers and analyze data to unearth potential risks, employing quantitative and qualitative methodologies to model and evaluate potential threats.

The GRC 20/20 blog succinctly sums up who a CRO is:

> *"The CRO holds the baton of risk management, conducting the different sections of risks to create a balanced and harmonious performance. Just as a conductor has a deep understanding of music and the unique characteristics of each instrument, the CRO possesses an in-depth knowledge of various risk types and how they interact within the organizational framework."*

Compliance Officers, on the other hand, stand as guardians of legal and regulatory adherence. Their responsibilities span ensuring the organization operates ethically and aligns with both external laws and internal policies. Within the financial sector, Credit Risk Analysts assess creditworthiness, determining the likelihood of default and managing the institution's exposure to credit-related risks.

Operational Risk Managers focus on internal processes, systems, and people, mitigating risks associated with technology, human error, and operational failures. In the realm of cybersecurity, Information Security Risk Managers stand sentinel, identifying and mitigating risks related to data security, protecting organizations from unauthorized access and cyber threats.

Insurance Risk Managers specialize in evaluating risks related to underwriting policies, establishing pricing structures commensurate with risk levels. Enterprise Risk Managers adopt a holistic approach, considering risks across all facets of an organization. They integrate risk management into strategic planning and decision-making processes, fostering a unified risk-aware culture.

Project Risk Managers, on the other hand, concentrate on risks associated with specific projects. Their goal is to ensure that potential pitfalls are identified and mitigated, facilitating the successful completion of projects. These roles collectively contribute to the creation of a risk-aware culture, the implementation of effective risk mitigation strategies, and the proactive addressing of challenges within the organization's operating environment. In the dynamic landscape of risk management, these professionals serve as stewards, navigating uncertainties and enabling organizations to thrive amidst complexity.

II. Compliance Specialists

These are professionals with expertise in compliance, including compliance officers, auditors, and legal professionals well-versed in regulatory requirements.

Compliance specialists are the vigilant guardians of organizational integrity, entrusted with the crucial task of ensuring that entities adhere to a labyrinth of laws, regulations, and internal policies. Serving as architects of internal policies, these specialists craft frameworks that align with legal requirements and industry standards, providing a blueprint for ethical conduct.

In their role as risk mitigators, compliance specialists identify and address potential pitfalls associated with non-compliance, acting as sentinels against legal and regulatory risks that could jeopardize an organization's reputation and financial stability. Their expertise extends to interpreting complex regulatory frameworks, translating intricate guidelines into actionable directives for the entire organization.

Through systematic audits and assessments, compliance specialists become auditors of organizational processes, verifying that these processes align with established policies and regulatory standards. They function as educators and communicators, disseminating information on regulatory changes, internal policies, and ethical considerations, nurturing a culture of awareness and understanding within the organization.

Upholding ethical standards is a fundamental tenet of their role, as compliance specialists champion ethical behavior, reinforcing an organization's commitment to integrity, transparency, and responsible business practices. In times of crisis or non-compliance issues, these specialists don multiple hats as crisis responders, working diligently to rectify issues, liaise with regulatory authorities, and implement corrective actions to restore compliance.

Embracing technology, compliance specialists integrate digital tools for efficient compliance management. They implement compliance management systems, automate processes, and leverage data analytics to enhance the effectiveness of compliance initiatives. Collaborating with senior management, these specialists offer strategic advice on navigating the complex regulatory landscape, providing insights on how compliance efforts align with the organization's strategic objectives and long-term sustainability.

It then becomes easy to see why this set of professionals will thrive in a GRC environment.

III. IT and Cybersecurity Experts

Professionals with a background in information technology, cybersecurity, or data protection. GRC roles often involve managing IT risks and ensuring data security and compliance.

In the complex and ever-evolving realms of information technology and cybersecurity, experts in these fields stand as digital guardians, tirelessly working to secure organizations against the myriad threats lurking in the digital landscape. Assuming the role of architects, they design and fortify digital systems with robust security protocols, encryption standards, and access controls, creating a resilient defense against cyber threats.

As adept threat detectives, these professionals are constantly vigilant, monitoring for signs of malicious activities. Armed with advanced tools and technologies, they detect, analyze, and respond to cyber threats with a proactive stance, ensuring that potential security breaches are identified and addressed swiftly.

Champions of security compliance, IT and cybersecurity experts navigate the intricate landscape of cybersecurity regulations. They ensure that organizations adhere to industry standards, legal requirements, and best practices, mitigating risks and steering clear of legal ramifications in an environment where compliance is paramount.

When cyber incidents occur, these experts seamlessly transition into incident responders. Investigating security breaches, containing the impact, and implementing remediation measures, they serve as the first line of defense, minimizing potential damage caused by cyber attacks and restoring normalcy.

As custodians of data encryption, they implement robust encryption protocols to safeguard sensitive information. Even in the event of a breach, the compromised data remains indecipherable, adding an extra layer of protection to the organization's digital assets.

Beyond their technical roles, IT and cybersecurity experts embrace the responsibility of educators. They disseminate knowledge on cybersecurity best practices, conduct training programs, and raise awareness among employees, fostering a pervasive culture of cyber hygiene within the organization.

In a proactive approach, these professionals often assume the role of ethical hackers. Conducting penetration testing and vulnerability assessments, they identify and address potential weaknesses in systems before malicious actors can exploit them, staying one step ahead of evolving cyber threats.

Embracing cutting-edge technologies, IT and cybersecurity experts integrate advanced tools into their arsenal. Intrusion detection systems, firewalls, and artificial intelligence-based security solutions are deployed to stay ahead in the ever-changing landscape of cyber threats.

Collaborating with organizational leadership, IT and cybersecurity experts offer strategic advice. Their insights contribute to cybersecurity strategy, risk management, and the integration of security measures into the overall business strategy. They align technology with organizational goals, ensuring that digital environments are not only secure but also in harmony with broader business objectives.

With this range of skillset, people in this line can easily pivot into GRC.

IV. Audit and Assurance Professionals

Auditors, internal or external, who possess a strong understanding of organizational processes and control frameworks.

Audit and assurance professionals emerge as the guardians of financial integrity, undertaking a critical role in ensuring the accuracy, transparency, and compliance of financial information. In their capacity as financial detectives, these experts meticulously explore the intricacies of financial records, leaving no aspect unchecked to verify balances and investigate any discrepancies that may arise.

Operating as compliance custodians, audit and assurance professionals ensure that financial statements align with applicable laws, regulations, and accounting standards. Their role extends beyond a mere examination of financial records; they become risk assessors, evaluating the potential for material misstatements in financial statements and offering insights into areas of vulnerability that might necessitate risk mitigation strategies.

Beyond their role as assurance providers, these professionals function as internal control evaluators, scrutinizing the effectiveness of systems designed to safeguard assets and ensure operational efficiency. Their assessments contribute significantly to the enhancement of internal control environments.

In the realm of financial advice, audit and assurance professionals provide recommendations for process improvements and internal control enhancements. They leverage their in-depth understanding of an organization's financial landscape to offer strategic insights that go beyond mere compliance.

Taking on the role of fraud examiners, these professionals employ forensic accounting techniques to detect and prevent fraudulent activities, contributing to the safeguarding of organizations from financial misconduct. They also serve as communicators, distilling complex financial information into comprehensible insights for various stakeholders, facilitating informed decision-making.

Embracing technological advancements, audit and assurance professionals integrate data analytics and audit automation tools into their processes. This ensures that audits are not only efficient but also capable of providing a more in-depth analysis of financial data.

As advocates for continuous improvement, these professionals stay abreast of industry trends, regulatory changes, and emerging risks. They adapt audit methodologies to meet the evolving needs of organizations, ensuring that their role remains dynamic and responsive to the challenges of the financial landscape.

In essence, audit and assurance professionals play multifaceted roles, serving as financial watchdogs and contributors to the overall financial health and governance of organizations. As a result, they can seamlessly switch to a career in GRC.

V. Legal and Ethics Professionals

Legal experts and professionals well-versed in ethical standards who can ensure that organizations operate within legal boundaries and adhere to ethical principles.

Legal and ethics professionals stand as stalwarts at the intersection of law and morality, playing indispensable roles in shaping organizational conduct. As guardians of legal compliance, these professionals meticulously interpret and apply laws and regulations, ensuring that every facet of organizational activity adheres to legal requirements, thus mitigating the risk of legal entanglements.

In the capacity of ethical advisers, these professionals provide invaluable guidance on navigating moral complexities. They assist organizations in making decisions anchored in ethical principles, fostering a culture where integrity and ethical considerations are not merely emphasized but are integral to decision-making processes.

Often serving as legal advocates, these professionals represent organizations in legal matters, handling contracts, negotiations, and potentially litigation to safeguard organizational interests. They become custodians of compliance, overseeing adherence to internal policies, industry standards, and ethical guidelines, constructing frameworks that encourage lawful and ethical conduct.

Risk mitigation is a key aspect of their roles, where legal and ethics professionals identify potential legal and ethical pitfalls. From contract disputes to ethical breaches, they develop strategies to navigate these challenges, shielding the organization from potential legal and reputational harm.

As policy architects, they contribute to the creation of guidelines that define acceptable conduct. Drafting policies that encapsulate legal requirements and ethical principles, they provide a roadmap for organizational behavior. Additionally, in the realm of conflict resolution, legal professionals may take on roles as mediators or arbitrators, facilitating negotiations and offering resolutions to disputes.

Education is a significant facet of their work, where these professionals serve as educators on legal and ethical standards. Through training programs, they ensure that employees not only understand but also adhere to legal requirements and ethical principles. Contributing to effective corporate governance, they provide advice on governance structures, director responsibilities, and disclosure requirements, ensuring transparency and accountability.

In the realm of technology integration, legal professionals embrace legaltech tools to enhance efficiency. Utilizing digital solutions for legal research, contract management, and compliance tracking, they stay at the forefront of technological advancements in the legal field.

In other words, legal and ethics professionals serve as custodians of organizational integrity, weaving a tapestry where legal compliance and ethical considerations are seamlessly integrated. Their multifaceted role makes them a perfect fit for GRC.

VI. Finance and Accounting Professionals

Individuals with financial backgrounds who can understand and manage financial risks, ensure financial compliance, and contribute to overall governance.

In the intricate tapestry of organizational success, finance and accounting professionals emerge as custodians of the financial realm. Their pivotal role revolves around managing financial records with precision, ensuring the accuracy and integrity of an organization's fiscal health. As strategic advisers, these experts delve into financial intricacies, offering insights that guide strategic decision-making. They navigate the financial landscape with a keen eye, serving as architects of budgets that efficiently allocate resources and align with overarching organizational objectives.

Beyond mere number-crunching, finance and accounting professionals champion compliance, diligently ensuring that financial statements adhere to stringent accounting standards and regulatory requirements. They don the hat of risk managers, identifying potential financial pitfalls and crafting strategies to mitigate risks, thereby contributing to the development of robust risk management policies.

These professionals transform into financial analysts, dissecting trends and performance metrics to provide data-driven insights that drive critical decisions in areas such as investments, cost management, and revenue generation. As adept financial reporters, they distill complex financial information into transparent and comprehensible statements, offering stakeholders a clear snapshot of an organization's fiscal health.

During audits, finance and accounting professionals become facilitators, collaborating seamlessly with auditors to ensure a smooth and transparent auditing process. They strategize on tax matters, optimizing positions within the framework of tax laws and developing tax-efficient strategies that maximize financial benefits.

Embracing the digital era, finance professionals integrate cutting-edge technologies into their workflows. Leveraging accounting software, data analytics, and financial modeling tools, they streamline processes and enhance the accuracy of financial reporting.

So, these professionals don't merely balance books; they shape the financial narrative of an organization. Their skills are certainly in need in the GRC terrain. In fact, need is an understatement, they are in premium demand.

VII. Project Managers

Project management professionals who can integrate GRC principles into project planning and execution, ensuring alignment with organizational goals.

Project managers, the unsung heroes of project execution, embody the essence of strategic orchestration and effective leadership. At the genesis of a project, they assume the role of visionaries, meticulously defining scope and objectives in collaboration with stakeholders, ensuring that the project aligns seamlessly with the overarching goals of the organization.

As strategic planners, project managers craft intricate roadmaps that delineate tasks, timelines, and resource requirements. They become resource orchestrators, skillfully allocating and managing resources to empower team members with the tools and support needed for optimal task execution.

In the role of team leaders, project managers cultivate collaborative environments, motivating team members to contribute their utmost to the project's success. Effective communication is their cornerstone, as they relay project goals, expectations, and progress transparently to stakeholders, fostering alignment and understanding.

As adept risk managers, project managers anticipate and mitigate potential roadblocks, steering the project through unforeseen challenges with resilience. They embody the essence of problem-solvers, addressing issues promptly to prevent minor setbacks from derailing overall progress.

Champions of quality assurance, project managers establish and monitor stringent standards, conducting regular evaluations to ensure that project deliverables meet predefined criteria. Custodians of the budget, they manage project finances meticulously, allocating resources judiciously to achieve objectives without exceeding constraints.

In the dynamic realm of project management, continuous learning is their mantra. Project managers stay abreast of industry trends, emerging technologies, and best practices, refining their skills to adapt to evolving methodologies and guarantee project success.

In essence, project managers are the linchpin of project triumph, seamlessly weaving together strategic planning, resource management, effective communication, and problem-solving. They would have no problem pivoting to GRC should they be interested.

VIII. Business Analysts

Those skilled in business analysis, who can analyze and optimize organizational processes to enhance governance and compliance.

In the intricate landscape of organizational dynamics, business analysts emerge as adept interpreters, translating the diverse and intricate needs of business stakeholders into a language comprehensible to IT teams. Their foundational role lies in meticulously architecting requirements, documenting intricate specifications that form the backbone of IT solutions.

Functioning as liaisons, business analysts bridge the communication gap between business stakeholders and IT teams, ensuring a harmonious collaboration that aligns organizational goals. They delve into the intricacies of organizational workflows as process analysts, identifying inefficiencies and proposing improvements to streamline operations.

Beyond interpreting business needs, these professionals wield data as a powerful tool for analysis and decision-making. They navigate the realm of data interpretation, extracting meaningful insights, and leveraging information to inform recommendations and drive business decisions.

As solution designers, business analysts collaborate with IT teams to craft solutions that not only address business challenges but also align with overarching objectives. They champion change management, assessing the impact of proposed changes and developing strategies for seamless implementation while advocating for user-centric design to enhance overall satisfaction.

In the face of challenges, business analysts step into the role of problem-solvers, analyzing complex issues and implementing strategies to optimize business processes. They are champions of continuous improvement, perpetually staying attuned to industry trends and evolving business needs to ensure that solutions remain relevant and effective.

IX. Quality Assurance Professionals

Quality assurance specialists who understand the importance of quality management and compliance within organizational processes.

Quality assurance professionals, the vigilant custodians of organizational standards, stand at the forefront of ensuring that products and services embody excellence. Serving as architects of meticulous testing processes, they design comprehensive strategies, scrutinizing everything from functionality to user experience, with the overarching goal of validating and guaranteeing the highest quality outcomes.

In their pursuit of quality, these professionals act as defenders of the user experience, ensuring that not only the functionality but also the usability of products and services align with customer expectations. Their role extends to that of diligent detectives, meticulously identifying and documenting defects, collaborating closely with development teams to rectify issues promptly, and enhance the overall quality of deliverables.

Functioning as auditors of processes, quality assurance professionals assess and optimize workflows to ensure efficiency and effectiveness. Embracing a continuous improvement mindset, they champion iterative enhancements, analyzing testing processes, gathering feedback, and implementing improvements to elevate the overall quality of products and services.

Risk mitigation is a core responsibility, where these professionals assess potential risks to product quality and implement strategies to ensure the reliability and resilience of deliverables. Acting as facilitators in collaborative efforts, they work closely with development teams, project managers, and stakeholders, aligning quality objectives with overarching project goals.

Navigating regulatory landscapes, quality assurance professionals ensure compliance with industry standards and regulations, establishing processes that mitigate the risk of legal and regulatory issues. Ultimately, they are advocates for customer satisfaction, ensuring that the final product or service not only meets specifications but surpasses customer expectations, thereby fostering loyalty and positive brand perception.

In short, quality assurance professionals would find GRC an interesting discipline to switch to as their skills give them a seamless transition.

X. Data Analysts and Scientists

Individuals with skills in data analysis and data science can contribute to risk assessment, predictive modeling, and decision-making processes.

In the realm of modern data alchemy, data analysts and scientists emerge as skilled interpreters, navigating the vast landscape of raw data to distill valuable insights. Their roles extend beyond mere number-crunching; they are statistical wizards, employing advanced statistical methods to unveil patterns and trends that form the foundation for informed decision-making.

As pioneers in programming, these professionals leverage coding expertise in languages like Python, R, or SQL to manipulate and analyze data efficiently. Their programming prowess allows them to automate processes, extract insights from complex datasets, and pave the way for efficient data-driven decision support.

Beyond the numerical realm, data analysts and scientists become storytellers, crafting narratives that translate complex data findings into compelling stories accessible to stakeholders across all organizational levels. They are predictive analysts, constructing models that forecast future trends, empowering organizations to proactively respond to emerging opportunities and challenges.

In the intricate landscape of machine learning, these professionals navigate complex algorithms, developing models that learn from data patterns. These models contribute to automation, pattern recognition, and the establishment of advanced decision support systems.

Champions of data quality assurance, data analysts and scientists ensure the accuracy and reliability of data. They implement rigorous processes to validate and clean datasets, ensuring that insights are rooted in trustworthy information. Their role as cross-disciplinary collaborators involves working closely with business leaders, IT professionals, and other stakeholders to align data initiatives with overarching organizational goals and strategies.

Embracing a commitment to continuous learning, data analysts and scientists stay abreast of new tools, technologies, and methodologies, ensuring that their skills remain at the forefront of the rapidly advancing data landscape. Ethical considerations are paramount in their work, as they act as stewards of data ethics, ensuring compliance with privacy regulations and upholding the highest standards of data integrity.

GRC will also be an enticing field of interest for data analysts and scientists.

XI. Corporate Governance Experts

Professionals with a background in corporate governance, including company secretaries, board members, and governance consultants.

In the intricate tapestry of organizational dynamics, corporate governance experts emerge as architects of ethical integrity and accountability. At the core of their responsibilities lies the crafting and upholding of ethical frameworks, establishing codes of conduct that lay the foundation for a culture of integrity within the organization.

As guardians of accountability, these professionals meticulously oversee reporting structures and frameworks, ensuring that individuals and entities are held responsible for their actions. They navigate the complex landscape of regulations, becoming custodians of compliance, and ensuring the organization operates within legal boundaries to mitigate the risk of legal and regulatory issues.

Risk management becomes a cornerstone of their role, as they identify and mitigate potential threats to the organization's stability and reputation, implementing strategies that ensure resilience in the face of uncertainties. Advocates for transparency, corporate governance experts ensure that information is disseminated in a clear and accessible manner, fostering trust through accurate and timely communication.

Facilitating the functioning of the board of directors, these experts optimize board performance by ensuring effective communication between the board and executive management, fostering collaboration and strategic alignment. They become engagement experts, actively involving shareholders and providing avenues for their input, contributing to a well-informed and engaged shareholder base.

In times of crisis, corporate governance experts step into leadership roles, developing crisis management strategies that uphold ethical conduct and stakeholder trust. Embracing a commitment to continuous improvement, they champion enhancements to governance structures, aligning processes with evolving best practices.

Beyond policies and structures, corporate governance experts serve as cultural ambassadors, fostering a governance culture that values ethical behavior, integrity, and responsible business practices. In essence, they are the custodians of organizational integrity, weaving a fabric that ensures ethical conduct, accountability, and transparency, contributing significantly to the organization's long-term sustainability and success.

XII. Health and Safety Professionals

Those with expertise in health and safety management who can contribute to risk management and compliance in industries with strict safety regulations.

In the ecosystem of organizational well-being, GRC inclusive, health and safety professionals emerge as guardians, meticulously curating workplaces that prioritize the safety and health of employees. At the heart of their responsibilities lies a commitment to risk assessment, where they pioneer efforts to identify and mitigate potential hazards, ensuring that workplaces are secure environments.

As compliance custodians, these professionals navigate the intricate landscape of safety regulations, ensuring that organizations adhere to legal requirements. They become leaders in emergency response, developing comprehensive plans to safeguard employees in times of crisis and ensuring that organizations are well-prepared to handle unforeseen events.

Advocates for ongoing training and education, health and safety professionals empower employees with the knowledge and skills necessary for maintaining a safe working environment. In incident investigations, they assume the role of experts, conducting thorough analyses to understand the root causes of incidents and developing strategies to prevent their recurrence.

Beyond safety, these professionals become ambassadors for health promotion, implementing programs and initiatives that address both physical and mental well-being. Nurturing a safety culture becomes integral to their work, fostering an environment where employees actively participate in safety initiatives and contribute to a culture of continuous improvement.

Advocating for the use of Personal Protective Equipment (PPE), health and safety professionals ensure that employees have access to and correctly use safety gear. They champion the implementation and enforcement of PPE policies, reducing the risk of workplace injuries and enhancing overall safety.

In their role as continuous improvement champions, health and safety professionals analyze incidents and feedback to enhance safety measures continually. They stay abreast of industry best practices, technology, and regulations to ensure that safety protocols remain effective and aligned with the evolving landscape.

This array of significance makes health and safety professionals highly invaluable to any sector or organisation, including GRC.

XIII. Environmental Management Professionals

Individuals with knowledge of environmental regulations and sustainable practices, contributing to compliance efforts and risk management related to environmental impact.

Environmental management professionals are stewards of ecological well-being, crafting strategies to align business activities with sustainability principles and navigate the complex realm of environmental regulations.

At the heart of their responsibilities lies a commitment to environmental sustainability. These professionals act as guardians, implementing strategies to assess, monitor, and enhance the environmental performance of organizations, with a goal to minimize ecological impact.

Navigating the intricate landscape of environmental regulations, these experts become compliance custodians, ensuring that organizations adhere to laws governing environmental practices. Through comprehensive environmental impact assessments, they analyze the potential effects of organizational activities, developing mitigation strategies and promoting sustainable practices.

Environmental management professionals are advocates for sustainable practices, exploring and recommending eco-friendly initiatives to minimize the ecological footprint of business operations. They strategically address waste management, developing plans to reduce waste generation, promote recycling, and ensure responsible disposal.

Focusing on conservation, these professionals become stewards of biodiversity, implementing programs to protect and enhance natural ecosystems. They also serve as educators and communicators, engaging stakeholders to raise awareness about environmental issues and promote responsible behavior.

With a focus on renewable energy, environmental management professionals advocate for and implement strategies to integrate sustainable energy sources into organizational operations, reducing reliance on non-renewable resources.

As analysts of carbon footprint, they assess and mitigate the environmental impact of organizations, developing strategies to minimize greenhouse gas emissions and contribute to the global effort to combat climate change.

Embracing continuous improvement, these professionals regularly analyze environmental performance, seeking innovative solutions and staying abreast of emerging technologies and best practices to enhance the sustainability of organizational practices.

All these make them the kind of professionals a perfect fit for GRC.

XIV. Ethical Hackers and Security Experts

Cybersecurity professionals, ethical hackers, and security experts who can assess and enhance the security of organizational systems and data.

In the vast and dynamic landscape of digital security, ethical hackers and security experts emerge as the vigilant guardians of virtual realms, entrusted with the crucial mission of fortifying information systems, networks, and data against malicious intrusions. With a skill set honed in the art of cybersecurity, these professionals play a pivotal role in identifying vulnerabilities, fortifying defenses, and ensuring the integrity of digital landscapes.

At the forefront of cybersecurity, ethical hackers are pioneers of digital guardianship. Their role transcends traditional security measures as they proactively seek vulnerabilities within information systems. Armed with a deep understanding of hacking techniques, they function as vulnerability assessment specialists, systematically analyzing systems to identify weaknesses that could potentially be exploited by cyber threats.

Distinguished as "white-hat" hackers, these cybersecurity professionals utilize their skills for ethical purposes. They conduct simulated cyberattacks, known as penetration testing, to identify and address vulnerabilities before malicious actors can exploit them. In the capacity of cybersecurity architects, they design and implement robust security frameworks, creating layered defense mechanisms to safeguard digital assets.

In times of cyber incidents, ethical hackers become incident response leaders. They develop and execute strategies to contain and mitigate the impact of breaches, working diligently to restore normalcy while minimizing damage. Acknowledging the human element in cybersecurity, they also serve as advocates for security awareness, designing training programs to educate employees about cybersecurity best practices.

With a keen focus on data protection, ethical hackers delve into cryptography, implementing and managing encryption protocols to safeguard sensitive information. They conduct penetration tests to simulate real-world cyberattacks, evaluating the resilience of systems and providing recommendations to enhance security posture.

Embracing the ever-evolving nature of cybersecurity, ethical hackers are continuous learning champions. They stay abreast of the latest hacking techniques, emerging threats, and technological advancements to ensure that their skills remain at the forefront of the cybersecurity landscape. In the aftermath of security incidents, these professionals transition into digital forensic analysts, meticulously investigating cybercrimes, analyzing digital evidence, and collaborating with law enforcement to bring cybercriminals to justice.

In essence, ethical hackers and security experts embody the frontline defenders of the digital realm and this makes them appropriate for the GRC universe.

XV. Communication and Public Relations Specialists

Professionals skilled in communication and public relations who can manage the reputational aspects of GRC, especially during times of crisis.

In the intricate realm of organizational communication, communication and public relations specialists emerge as the architects of reputation, diligently crafting narratives and fostering meaningful connections with diverse audiences. Their pivotal role revolves around shaping compelling stories that mirror the organization's values and achievements, influencing perceptions positively.

As brand ambassadors, these specialists embody the essence of the organization, tirelessly working to build and maintain a favorable brand image. Their responsibilities extend to becoming adept media liaisons, nurturing relationships with various media outlets, influencers, and journalists to ensure positive coverage and adeptly managing crisis communication when required.

During crises, these professionals transform into crisis communication experts, strategizing transparent and effective communication to mitigate reputational damage and maintain stakeholder trust. In the digital era, they seamlessly navigate the landscape as content creators and curators, producing engaging content across platforms to maintain a consistent organizational voice.

Facilitating meaningful stakeholder engagement, communication specialists build and nurture relationships with a broad spectrum of stakeholders. This includes customers, employees, investors, and the community, tailoring communication to each audience for a personalized and impactful approach.

In the realm of social media dominance, these professionals serve as adept social media managers, navigating platforms, curating engaging content, and actively participating in online conversations. As communication strategists, they develop comprehensive communication plans aligned with organizational objectives, leveraging trends and opportunities for positive exposure.

Safeguarding organizational reputation becomes a core responsibility. These specialists proactively manage perceptions, address misconceptions, and work diligently to ensure the organization's reputation remains positive and resilient. Embracing the dynamic nature of their field, they serve as advocates for continuous learning, staying abreast of industry trends, emerging technologies, and best practices to ensure their strategies remain innovative and effective.

In essence, communication and public relations specialists are the stewards of organizational communication, using their skills to shape narratives, engage stakeholders, and navigate the complexities of the ever-evolving media landscape. Through their strategic approach, they can contribute significantly to the success of any GRC-inclined organisation.

XVI. Leaders and Decision-Makers

Executives, directors, and leaders who recognize the strategic importance of effective governance, risk management, and compliance in achieving organizational objectives.

In the intricate landscape of Governance, Risk, and Compliance (GRC), leaders and decision-makers emerge as architects of organizational integrity, steering the course towards a culture of accountability and ethical decision-making. Their influence is profound, shaping the ethos of the organization and embedding principles of governance, risk management, and compliance into the fabric of its operations.

At the helm, leaders set the tone at the top, establishing a paradigm that prioritizes ethical behavior, regulatory compliance, and vigilant risk management. This commitment ripples through the organization, shaping the attitudes and actions of every stakeholder.

Decision-makers, often represented by executive leadership and boards of directors, play a crucial role in defining the organization's risk appetite. They determine the threshold of risk acceptable in pursuit of strategic objectives, laying the foundation for robust risk management practices.

Strategic alignment becomes a focal point, with leaders ensuring that GRC initiatives seamlessly integrate with the overarching organizational strategy. Decisions related to governance structures, risk frameworks, and compliance programs are made with a strategic lens, fostering resilience and long-term value creation.

Resource allocation for GRC initiatives is a decision-makers' responsibility, recognizing the need to invest in systems, personnel, and training that fortify governance structures, enhance risk management capabilities, and ensure compliance with regulatory frameworks.

The integration of GRC into decision-making processes becomes a hallmark of leadership. Leaders consider the implications of decisions on governance, compliance, and risk, ensuring that GRC considerations are integral to both strategic and operational choices.

Oversight and accountability are paramount responsibilities. Decision-makers exercise vigilant oversight, holding individuals and departments accountable for GRC outcomes. This involves monitoring the implementation of policies, assessing risk mitigation efforts, and ensuring adherence to applicable laws and regulations.

Communication and transparency stand as pillars of leadership in the GRC context. Leaders communicate expectations related to GRC to all stakeholders, fostering a culture of openness and accountability. This commitment to transparency builds trust and reinforces the importance of ethical conduct.

Responding to emerging risks requires agility. Leaders and decision-makers adapt GRC strategies to address new challenges, leveraging their strategic vision to guide the organization through evolving risk landscapes and unforeseen circumstances.

Continuous improvement is championed by leaders who encourage learning from incidents, conduct regular assessments of GRC processes, and promote innovation to enhance the effectiveness of governance, risk management, and compliance initiatives.

Ethical leadership becomes a guiding principle. Leaders model ethical behavior and integrity, emphasizing the significance of ethical decision-making in all facets of the organization. This commitment sets the tone for an ethical culture, a cornerstone of effective GRC.

In sum, leaders and decision-makers shape the destiny of GRC within an organization. Their commitment, strategic acumen, and active involvement in GRC processes are fundamental to navigating risks, ensuring compliance, and fostering a culture of ethical and responsible conduct.

XVII. Continuous Learners and Adapters

Individuals who embrace a mindset of continuous learning and adaptation, as the GRC landscape is dynamic and subject to regulatory changes.

These individuals serve as the sentinels of regulatory knowledge, diligently staying informed about changes in regulations. Their commitment ensures that the organization remains nimble, swiftly adjusting policies and procedures to align with the latest legal frameworks, thus maintaining a posture of continuous compliance.

As pioneers of technological progress in the GRC sphere, adapters eagerly embrace cutting-edge tools and methodologies. Their continuous learning ethos equips the organization with the latest technological advancements, empowering effective risk assessment, compliance monitoring, and governance processes.

They play a vital role in dynamic risk assessment, proactively staying informed about emerging risks. This forward-thinking approach enhances the organization's adaptability, allowing for agile adjustments to risk management strategies in response to evolving threats and uncertainties.

Actively seeking and implementing best practices, these individuals are champions of continuous improvement in GRC. Their commitment propels the adoption of industry-leading approaches, refining governance structures, risk management processes, and compliance initiatives to achieve optimal outcomes.

In the realm of training and awareness, continuous learners are pivotal, ensuring that employees understand their roles in upholding compliance, managing risks, and contributing to effective governance. Their knowledge dissemination fosters a culture where GRC principles are not just known but embraced.

As experts in process optimization, these individuals leverage their adaptability to identify inefficiencies and propose improvements. Their continuous improvement mindset elevates the overall effectiveness of governance, risk management, and compliance initiatives, ensuring operational excellence.

In times of crisis, continuous learners and adapters shine as agile crisis managers. Their ability to swiftly assimilate new information and adjust strategies positions the organization to respond effectively to unforeseen challenges, minimizing the impact of crises on the GRC framework.

They actively foster a learning culture within the organization, championing continuous education and adaptability. This advocacy creates a workplace where staying informed about GRC practices is not merely encouraged but valued, fostering a resilient and responsive organizational ethos.

As monitors of industry trends, continuous learners keep a vigilant eye on emerging methodologies and evolving standards in GRC. Their awareness empowers the organization to proactively align with best practices, ensuring a forward-looking GRC approach that anticipates and adapts to industry shifts.

In navigating cultural changes related to GRC, adapters play a crucial role. Their adaptability helps smooth the transition, whether introducing new compliance measures or fostering a risk-aware culture, ensuring that employees embrace the evolving GRC landscape with understanding and commitment.

In essence, continuous learners and adapters are the driving force behind a resilient and adaptive GRC ecosystem. Their commitment to perpetual learning and adaptability fortifies the organization, enabling it to navigate complexities, embrace change, and maintain a robust and effective GRC framework.

XVIII. Problem Solvers

People with strong problem-solving skills who can navigate complex issues, make informed decisions, and contribute to the resolution of challenges related to governance, risk, and compliance.

People without significant technical skills can absolutely venture into Governance, Risk, and Compliance (GRC). GRC is a diverse field that embraces professionals from various backgrounds. Individuals with legal, compliance, finance, risk management, business analysis, corporate governance, communication, and environmental health and safety expertise, among others, can make valuable contributions to GRC efforts. Leadership roles and decision-makers who recognize the strategic importance of GRC and continuous learners with a commitment to staying informed are also highly valuable in the field. The key is to leverage existing skills, cultivate a broad understanding of GRC principles, and adapt to the evolving landscape of governance, risk management, and compliance.

As adept risk identifiers and analysts, problem solvers bring a discerning eye to the GRC landscape, contributing to the comprehensive assessment of potential risks and vulnerabilities. Their keen ability to analyze and strategize proves invaluable in navigating the intricate terrain of risk management.

In the domain of compliance, problem solvers take center stage in resolving issues. Whether addressing non-compliance challenges or navigating the complexities of regulatory frameworks, their analytical skills come to the forefront, paving the way for effective and compliant solutions.

Actively engaging in the optimization of GRC processes, problem solvers meticulously analyze workflows, identifying inefficiencies, and proposing improvements. Their role is crucial in streamlining operations, ensuring that governance, risk management, and compliance processes operate with efficiency and effectiveness.

During times of crisis, problem solvers become linchpins in the GRC framework. Their ability to think strategically and devise solutions swiftly proves pivotal in mitigating the impact of crises, ensuring a resilient and effective response that aligns with organizational objectives.

In the capacity of decision support, problem solvers offer insights into complex GRC issues. They assist decision-makers in understanding the root causes of challenges, evaluating various solutions, and making informed decisions that align with the overarching objectives of the organization.

Engaging in thorough root cause analysis, problem solvers dissect issues to their core, identifying underlying factors contributing to problems. This approach facilitates the implementation of targeted and sustainable solutions, preventing the recurrence of challenges within the GRC framework.

Amid the ever-evolving technological landscape of GRC, problem solvers play a pivotal role in integrating and optimizing technology solutions. They assess compatibility, address integration challenges, and ensure that chosen tools align seamlessly with GRC goals, leveraging technology for enhanced efficiency.

Driving a culture of continuous improvement within GRC, problem solvers actively seek opportunities for enhancement. Their commitment to adopting best practices and implementing innovative solutions fosters an environment where GRC frameworks are not static but evolve to meet emerging challenges.

Facilitating collaboration among stakeholders, problem solvers bridge communication gaps and mediate conflicts, ensuring a cohesive and collaborative approach in addressing GRC challenges. Their role in fostering effective stakeholder collaboration contributes to the overall success of GRC initiatives.

Contributing to the training and education of GRC teams, problem solvers identify knowledge gaps, develop targeted training programs, and empower teams with the skills needed to proactively address challenges in governance, risk management, and compliance.

In essence, problem solvers bring a dynamic problem-solving mindset to the GRC arena, enhancing the adaptability, resilience, and overall effectiveness of organizations in navigating the complexities of governance, risk, and compliance.

3.2 Is going into GRC worth it?

Here comes the big question that could have remained unanswered despite reading this book to this point: is going into GRC worth it?

The thing is, the profitability of Governance, Risk, and Compliance (GRC) is not typically measured in the same way as traditional business ventures. Instead, the value of GRC lies in its ability to safeguard organizations from potential risks, enhance decision-making processes, ensure compliance with regulations, and protect against reputational damage. While GRC initiatives may not directly generate revenue, they contribute to the long-term sustainability and success of businesses by fostering a culture of transparency, accountability, and ethical conduct. Effectively implemented GRC practices can save organizations from financial losses due to legal issues, regulatory fines, and operational disruptions.

Embarking on a career in Governance, Risk, and Compliance (GRC) offers individuals a unique and rewarding path characterized by diverse opportunities and significant contributions to organizational success.

Here are compelling reasons why you should consider pursuing a career in GRC:

HOLISTIC UNDERSTANDING OF BUSINESS

A GRC career provides individuals with a comprehensive understanding of how organizations operate. It involves overseeing governance structures, managing risks, and ensuring compliance, offering a holistic perspective on business operations.

STRATEGIC DECISION-MAKING SKILLS

GRC professionals develop strong strategic decision-making skills. They learn to analyze complex situations, assess risks, and make informed decisions that align with organizational goals, contributing to effective leadership.

ENHANCING ORGANIZATIONAL RESILIENCE

GRC professionals play a vital role in enhancing organizational resilience. By identifying and managing risks, they contribute to the organization's ability to withstand challenges, adapt to change, and thrive in dynamic environments.

ETHICAL LEADERSHIP AND COMPLIANCE

GRC careers emphasize ethical leadership and compliance with regulatory frameworks. Individuals in this field cultivate a strong sense of integrity, ensuring that organizations adhere to legal and ethical standards in their operations.

DIVERSE CAREER OPPORTUNITIES

The GRC field offers diverse career opportunities across industries. Professionals can specialize in governance, risk management, compliance, or pursue roles that encompass all three areas. This versatility allows for career growth and specialization.

CONTRIBUTION TO ORGANIZATIONAL SUCCESS

GRC professionals directly contribute to organizational success by creating and maintaining frameworks that foster good governance, manage risks effectively, and ensure compliance with laws and regulations.

DYNAMIC AND EVOLVING FIELD

GRC is a dynamic and ever-evolving field. As new risks emerge and regulatory landscapes evolve, professionals in GRC are continuously engaged in learning and adapting, making it an exciting and intellectually stimulating career choice.

GLOBAL OPPORTUNITIES

GRC skills are transferable across borders, providing individuals with opportunities to work on a global scale. As businesses expand internationally, professionals with expertise in GRC are in demand to navigate diverse regulatory environments.

IN DEMAND ACROSS INDUSTRIES

GRC professionals are in demand across a wide range of industries, including finance, healthcare, technology, and more. This demand ensures a steady stream of job opportunities and career growth for individuals in the field.

CONTRIBUTION TO SUSTAINABILITY

GRC professionals contribute to the sustainability of organizations by identifying and mitigating risks that could impact long-term viability. This focus on sustainability aligns with the growing emphasis on corporate social responsibility and environmental, social, and governance (ESG) factors.

CONTINUOUS LEARNING AND DEVELOPMENT

GRC professionals are continually learning and adapting to new challenges. This commitment to ongoing education and skill development ensures that individuals stay at the forefront of industry best practices and remain valuable assets to their organizations.

3.3 What to know before embarking on the GRC journey

By now, you should be convinced that GRC is worth exploring. But before embarking on a journey into Governance, Risk, and Compliance (GRC), it's crucial to grasp several key considerations.

First, a foundational understanding of GRC components—Governance, Risk, and Compliance—is essential. This involves recognizing the significance of organizational structures, decision-making processes, risk management strategies, and adherence to legal and ethical standards. A fuller explanation had been done in previous sections.

Understanding the industry-specific regulatory landscape is equally vital. Each sector operates under distinct compliance requirements, and comprehending these regulations is pivotal for effective GRC implementation.

Educational qualifications or certifications related to GRC can enhance your knowledge base. Certifications such as CISA, CRISC, or CRMA are recognized in the GRC field and can validate your expertise.

While some technical skills might be beneficial, it's important to note that GRC roles are diverse and encompass various disciplines. Legal professionals, compliance specialists, risk management experts, finance professionals, and individuals with strong analytical or communication skills can all find meaningful roles in GRC.

Networking within the GRC community, seeking mentorship, and staying updated on industry news contribute to a well-rounded approach. Professionals in GRC should cultivate not only technical skills but also effective communication, critical thinking, and problem-solving abilities.

A continuous learning mindset is fundamental in GRC due to its dynamic nature. Being adaptable to industry changes, regulatory updates, and emerging risks ensures a proactive and effective approach to GRC practices.

4.4 Summarising the GRC Landscape

Introducing the GRC landscape involves unraveling the intricate interplay of Governance, Risk, and Compliance within organizational frameworks. At its core, governance establishes the structures and processes guiding decision-making, accountability, and ethical conduct. This foundational element sets the stage for effective risk management and compliance efforts.

Risk management, a pivotal aspect of the GRC landscape, revolves around identifying, assessing, and mitigating uncertainties that could impact organizational objectives. It requires a proactive approach to navigate challenges and capitalize on opportunities, ensuring resilience in the face of dynamic environments.

Compliance, the third pillar, mandates adherence to laws, regulations, and internal policies. It acts as a safeguard against legal issues and reputational damage, aligning organizational practices with ethical standards and regulatory requirements.

Navigating the GRC landscape requires a comprehensive understanding of these interconnected elements. Organizations must establish robust GRC frameworks that integrate governance, risk management, and compliance seamlessly. Leveraging technology plays a crucial role, with GRC software, data analytics, and automation tools streamlining processes and enhancing decision-making.

As GRC evolves, continuous monitoring, adaptability, and a commitment to best practices become paramount. Realizing the GRC landscape entails recognizing its strategic importance, aligning practices with organizational goals, and fostering a culture of transparency and accountability. In essence, introducing the GRC landscape unveils a holistic approach to organizational management, ensuring resilience, ethical conduct, and sustained success.

CHAPTER FOUR

DECODING GRC ESSENTIALS: A NON-TECH APPROACH

As a non-tech person venturing into GRC, you need to understand the essentials of Governance, Risk and Compliance. You have been introduced to the basic concepts in chapter one but this chapter does a fuller breakdown of GRC essentials.

The essentials of Governance, Risk, and Compliance (GRC) constitute a comprehensive framework that organizations employ to navigate the complexities of modern business environments. At its core, governance establishes the structures and processes guiding decision-making, accountability, and ethical conduct. It encompasses the delineation of responsibilities, ensuring that the organization operates in alignment with its objectives and values.

Risk management, a fundamental pillar of GRC, involves the systematic identification, assessment, and mitigation of uncertainties that could impact the achievement of organizational objectives. This proactive approach to risk ensures that organizations can navigate challenges, capitalize on opportunities, and maintain resilience in the face of a dynamic and uncertain landscape.

Compliance, the third crucial element, requires adherence to laws, regulations, and internal policies. It acts as a safeguard against legal issues, reputational damage, and financial losses. By aligning organizational practices with ethical standards and regulatory requirements, compliance forms a protective shield for the organization's integrity and stability.

In the realm of GRC, these three elements are intricately interlinked. Establishing a robust GRC framework involves integrating governance, risk management, and compliance seamlessly.

Technology plays a pivotal role, with organizations leveraging GRC software, data analytics, and automation tools to streamline processes, enhance decision-making, and ensure the effectiveness of their GRC initiatives.

As organizations evolve, the essentials of GRC demand continuous monitoring, adaptability to changing landscapes, and a commitment to best practices. Realizing the full potential of GRC necessitates recognizing its strategic importance, aligning practices with organizational goals, and fostering a culture of transparency and accountability. Ultimately, the basis of GRC provides a structured and holistic approach to organizational management, contributing to resilience, ethical conduct, and sustained success.

When considering GRC from a non-tech perspective, it emphasizes the need for well-defined organizational structures, clear decision-making processes, and a commitment to ethical conduct. It involves fostering a risk-aware culture that encourages proactive identification and management of potential challenges. Compliance, in this context, is about instilling a sense of responsibility for adhering to established standards and regulations.

In essence, the non-tech approach to GRC underscores the human and organizational aspects, focusing on effective governance structures, risk-aware decision-making, and a commitment to ethical behavior. While technology may enhance these processes, the essentials of GRC lie in the people, culture, and values that shape the organization.

4.1 BUILDING A GRC FRAMEWORK

Building a Governance, Risk, and Compliance (GRC) framework is a strategic journey that involves weaving together various elements to ensure the effective operation, proactive risk management, and regulatory compliance of an organization. At its core, this task entails creating a holistic system that considers the interconnected nature of governance, risk, and compliance within the organizational context.

Central to this framework is the establishment of robust governance structures. This includes defining the organization's hierarchy, roles, and responsibilities. By outlining clear lines of authority and decision-making processes, governance becomes the guiding force directing the organization's strategic trajectory.

A pivotal step in building a GRC framework is determining the organization's risk appetite and tolerance. This involves articulating the acceptable level of risk in pursuit of objectives, requiring a thorough understanding of the types of risks relevant to the business and their potential impact.

Identifying and assessing risks follows suit, demanding a meticulous analysis of internal and external factors that could impact the organization. Risks are categorized, and their potential impact and likelihood are evaluated, enabling prioritization and focused mitigation efforts.

Developing comprehensive policies and procedures is another critical aspect of the framework. These documents cover various areas, including ethical conduct, data protection, financial management, and compliance with laws and regulations. Clarity in these documents is paramount for effective implementation.

Risk mitigation strategies are then implemented based on the identified risks. This could involve process improvements, the introduction of control mechanisms, insurance strategies, or other proactive measures aimed at minimizing the likelihood and impact of potential risks.

Modern GRC frameworks integrate technology, automating processes, enabling real-time monitoring, and facilitating insightful analytics. This technological integration enhances the efficiency and effectiveness of GRC efforts.

Ensuring compliance mechanisms is vital, requiring organizations to stay abreast of relevant laws, regulations, and industry standards. Continuous monitoring, regular updates to policies, and mechanisms to track and demonstrate compliance are essential components.

Beyond structures and processes, building a GRC framework involves cultivating a culture of governance, risk awareness, and compliance throughout the organization. This requires ongoing training, communication, and instilling a sense of responsibility among employees at all levels.

A GRC framework is not static; it demands continuous monitoring and improvement. Regular assessments, audits, and feedback loops are essential to ensure the framework remains aligned with the organization's goals, adapts to changing circumstances, and addresses emerging risks.

To cap, building a GRC framework is a multifaceted endeavor that demands a strategic and integrated approach. By establishing strong governance structures, addressing risks, developing comprehensive policies, leveraging technology, and fostering a culture of compliance, organizations can create a resilient framework that not only mitigates risks but also contributes to sustained success in a dynamic business environment.

4.2 GRC Roles and Responsibilities

Within the Governance, Risk, and Compliance (GRC) framework, distinct roles and responsibilities are assigned to various individuals within an organization. These roles are crucial in ensuring that the organization operates ethically, manages risks effectively, and remains compliant with relevant laws and regulations.

I. Governance Roles

Board of Directors and Executive Leadership: The board and executive leadership hold primary governance responsibilities, setting the strategic direction, overseeing operations, and ensuring that decisions align with the organization's mission and values.

Chief Governance Officer (CGO): The CGO is responsible for coordinating governance activities, facilitating communication between the board and executive leadership, and ensuring that governance structures are effective and aligned with organizational goals.

II. Risk Management Roles

Chief Risk Officer (CRO): The CRO oversees the organization's risk management strategy, identifying potential risks, assessing their impact, and implementing mitigation strategies to safeguard the organization's assets and reputation.

Risk Management Team: This team works closely with the CRO to conduct risk assessments, monitor risk factors, and implement risk mitigation measures throughout the organization.

III. Compliance Roles

Chief Compliance Officer (CCO): The CCO is responsible for ensuring that the organization adheres to relevant laws, regulations, and internal policies. They lead compliance efforts, conduct audits, and develop strategies to address any compliance gaps.

Compliance Team: This team works under the CCO to monitor regulatory changes, conduct compliance assessments, and collaborate with various departments to implement and enforce compliance measures.

IV. Internal Control Roles

Chief Internal Auditor: The Chief Internal Auditor oversees internal audit functions, evaluating the effectiveness of internal controls, identifying areas for improvement, and ensuring that the organization's operations align with established standards and policies.

V. Technology and Data Governance Roles

Chief Information Security Officer (CISO): The CISO is responsible for managing and mitigating cybersecurity risks, ensuring the security of information assets, and implementing data governance strategies to protect sensitive data.

Data Governance Team: This team collaborates with the CISO to establish data governance policies, manage data quality, and ensure compliance with data protection regulations.

VI. Legal and Ethics Roles

General Counsel: The General Counsel oversees legal affairs, providing legal advice, drafting contracts, and ensuring that the organization operates within the boundaries of the law.

Ethics Officer: This role focuses on promoting ethical conduct within the organization, developing a code of ethics, and handling ethical concerns raised by employees.

VII. Corporate Compliance and Reporting Roles

Corporate Compliance Officer: This role focuses on ensuring that the organization complies with industry-specific regulations and standards, preparing compliance reports, and liaising with external regulatory bodies when necessary.

VIII. Training and Communication Roles

Training and Communication Officer: This role is responsible for developing and implementing training programs on governance, risk management, and compliance, ensuring that employees are aware of their responsibilities and stay informed about relevant changes.

To conclude, the roles and responsibilities within the GRC framework are diverse, involving individuals at various levels of the organization. Clear delineation of these roles ensures effective coordination, communication, and implementation of GRC strategies, ultimately contributing to the organization's success, resilience, and ethical operation in a complex business environment.

CHAPTER FIVE

IMPLEMENTING GRC TECHNOLOGIES

After you have learnt the rudiments of GRC and how to approach them even with your non-tech experience in the previous chapters, this chapter simplifies how to implement GRC technologies.

Implementing Governance, Risk, and Compliance (GRC) technologies marks a pivotal step for organizations seeking to fortify their operational resilience, enhance decision-making processes, and ensure compliance with regulatory requirements. In an era characterized by dynamic business landscapes and evolving regulatory frameworks, the integration of GRC technologies emerges as a strategic imperative, offering a comprehensive solution for managing the interconnected facets of governance, risk management, and compliance.

As Brenda Boultwood, Sr. VP, GRC Solutions said at the MetricStream #GRC Summit Europe 2014 in London, "...*GRC is maturing and it can bring significant savings to a company*."

At its core, GRC technology represents a sophisticated framework that leverages cutting-edge tools and platforms to streamline and automate processes associated with governance structures, risk assessment and management, and compliance tracking. This introduction delves into the key aspects of implementing GRC technologies, shedding light on the transformative impact they can have on organizational efficiency and effectiveness.

In the face of increasing complexities and uncertainties, organizations recognize the need for a unified approach to GRC. GRC technologies provide a centralized hub where governance, risk, and compliance functions converge, enabling a holistic view of the organization's operational landscape. This integrated perspective facilitates informed decision-making, as leaders gain real-time insights into potential risks, compliance status, and overall governance structures.

The deployment of GRC technologies is not merely a technological upgrade but a strategic initiative that aligns with the organization's overarching goals. These technologies offer a seamless fusion of governance, risk management, and compliance, creating synergies that go beyond individual functions. By automating routine tasks, generating actionable insights, and fostering collaboration across departments, GRC technologies empower organizations to proactively address challenges and capitalize on opportunities.

The implementation process involves configuring GRC platforms to align with the organization's specific needs and industry requirements. This customization ensures that the technology adapts to the unique risk landscape, compliance mandates, and governance structures of the organization. It involves mapping out workflows, defining risk tolerance thresholds, and establishing protocols for compliance tracking.

A fundamental aspect of implementing GRC technologies is the integration of data analytics. These technologies harness the power of data to provide organizations with predictive and prescriptive insights. By analyzing historical data, identifying patterns, and anticipating emerging risks, GRC technologies enable organizations to move beyond reactive risk management to a proactive stance, enhancing their ability to navigate uncertainties effectively.

As organizations embark on the implementation journey, considerations for user training and change management become paramount. Ensuring that employees at all levels are proficient in utilizing GRC technologies fosters a culture of transparency, accountability, and shared responsibility. Effective change management strategies help organizations navigate the transition smoothly, maximizing the benefits of GRC technology adoption.

5.1 Leveraging Technology for Governance

Leveraging technology for governance within the Governance, Risk, and Compliance (GRC) framework is instrumental in enhancing organizational effectiveness, transparency, and strategic decision-making. Technological advancements provide innovative tools and platforms that streamline governance processes, automate workflows, and enable real-time monitoring.

In the intricate realm of Governance, Risk, and Compliance (GRC), a spectrum of software solutions emerges as indispensable tools, fostering streamlined decision-making processes while bolstering accountability and transparency within organizations.

Enterprises harness Enterprise Risk Management (ERM) software to navigate the labyrinth of uncertainties. This tool not only identifies and assesses risks but also aligns risk management efforts with organizational goals, injecting a structured framework into the governance fabric. It paints a clear picture for decision-makers, allowing them to prioritize and tailor risk mitigation strategies. The accountability and transparency it affords stem from the ability to track risk ownership, offering a window into the status of risk management initiatives.

Compliance Management Software, another pillar in the GRC landscape, aids organizations in adhering to the ever-evolving landscape of regulations and standards. By centralizing compliance requirements and monitoring changes, it not only supports governance by ensuring consistent policy application but also acts as a beacon for accountability and transparency. The software becomes a sentinel, providing visibility into compliance status, audit trails, and documentation, thereby reinforcing the organization's commitment to regulatory obligations.

Policy Management Software steps onto the stage as the guardian of internal directives and procedures. In the governance arena, it assists in the creation, communication, and enforcement of policies, aligning them with organizational objectives. The software's impact on accountability and transparency is evident through its capacity to track policy acknowledgments, changes, and exceptions, ensuring a cohesive policy enforcement framework.

Audit Management Software takes the spotlight by orchestrating the entire audit lifecycle. It contributes to governance by offering a systematic approach to audits, ensuring their alignment with organizational goals and compliance requirements. This software, a sentinel of accountability and transparency, meticulously records audit findings, corrective actions, and progress, creating an audit trail that resonates with integrity and clarity.

The pinnacle of GRC software solutions lies in Governance, Risk, and Compliance Platforms (GRC Platforms). These comprehensive platforms amalgamate disparate GRC functions into a unified system, providing organizations with a panoramic view of their risk and compliance landscapes. Serving as a linchpin for governance, these platforms align risk and compliance activities with strategic objectives. Their impact on accountability and transparency reverberates through centralized reporting, dashboards, and analytics, offering organizations a lens through which to view and enhance GRC activities.

a. Integrated GRC Platforms

Centralized Data Management: Utilize integrated GRC platforms that centralize data related to governance structures, policies, and decision-making processes. This centralized approach ensures consistency, reduces redundancy, and provides a holistic view of governance activities.

b. Automation of Governance Processes

Workflow Automation: Implement workflow automation tools to streamline governance processes. Automation reduces manual efforts, minimizes the risk of errors, and ensures that governance-related tasks are executed efficiently.

c. **Decision Support Systems**

Data Analytics for Decision-Making: Employ data analytics tools to analyze governance data. This provides actionable insights for decision-makers, facilitating informed and data-driven decision-making in alignment with organizational objectives.

d. **Electronic Document Management**

Digital Documentation: Transition to electronic document management systems to facilitate the creation, storage, and retrieval of governance-related documents. This enhances accessibility, version control, and ensures that documentation is secure and easily auditable.

e. **Board Portals and Collaboration Tools**

Virtual Board Portals: Implement virtual board portals that enable secure collaboration among board members. These tools provide a centralized platform for sharing documents, conducting virtual meetings, and facilitating communication for efficient governance.

f. **Cybersecurity Measures**

Secure Information Sharing: Utilize cybersecurity measures to ensure secure information sharing within governance processes. Encryption, secure access controls, and regular cybersecurity assessments contribute to safeguarding sensitive governance data.

g. **Regulatory Compliance Tracking**

Regulatory Technology (RegTech): Leverage RegTech solutions to stay abreast of regulatory changes impacting governance. Automated compliance tracking tools can monitor regulatory updates, assess their impact, and facilitate prompt adjustments to governance processes.

h. Continuous Monitoring and Auditing

Continuous Monitoring Tools: Implement continuous monitoring tools that track changes in governance-related activities in real-time. This ensures ongoing compliance, identifies potential issues promptly, and facilitates proactive risk management.

i. Training and Awareness Programs

E-Learning Platforms: Utilize e-learning platforms and technology-driven training modules for governance education. This ensures that individuals involved in governance processes stay informed about best practices, ethical standards, and organizational policies.

j. Blockchain for Transparency

Blockchain Technology: Explore the use of blockchain technology for enhancing transparency in governance. Blockchain can provide an immutable and transparent record of governance-related transactions, ensuring accountability and trust.

k. Mobile Accessibility

Mobile Governance Apps: Provide mobile accessibility to governance-related information and processes. Mobile apps enable stakeholders, including board members and executives, to access critical governance data on the go, promoting flexibility and responsiveness.

5.2 Risk Management Tools and Techniques

In the dynamic landscape of contemporary business, navigating uncertainties and mitigating risks are imperative for organizational resilience. This chapter delves into the multifaceted realm of Risk Management Tools and Techniques, illuminating the array of technologies that serve as stalwart allies in the pursuit of effective risk identification, assessment, and monitoring.

5.2.1 Risk Identification Tools

Effective risk management commences with the art of identification, and organizations today are equipped with sophisticated tools to illuminate potential threats. Among the arsenal is the Risk Register, a digital repository that systematically captures and categorizes various risks. This tool acts as a sentinel, allowing organizations to proactively catalog risks and their attributes, providing a comprehensive foundation for subsequent risk analysis.

Furthermore, cutting-edge technologies, such as Artificial Intelligence (AI) and Machine Learning (ML), contribute significantly to risk identification. These technologies sift through vast datasets, uncovering patterns and anomalies that might elude traditional risk assessment methods. The amalgamation of human expertise and technological prowess enhances the efficacy of risk identification processes, enabling organizations to stay ahead of emerging threats.

5.2.2 Risk Assessment Techniques

Once risks are identified, the focus shifts to assessment, a critical phase in the risk management continuum. Quantitative and qualitative risk assessment techniques come to the fore, each playing a distinct role in evaluating the potential impact and likelihood of identified risks.

Quantitative techniques involve numerical analysis, employing tools like Monte Carlo Simulation to simulate various scenarios and gauge potential outcomes. On the qualitative front, tools such as Risk Matrix facilitate a more subjective evaluation, considering factors like severity and probability.

Risk assessment tools also embrace Scenario Analysis, enabling organizations to envision and evaluate potential future events. Through this technique, organizations gain a nuanced understanding of how risks may unfold, empowering them to develop targeted mitigation strategies.

5.2.3 Risk Monitoring Technologies

In the ever-evolving landscape of risks, continuous monitoring is imperative. Advanced technologies empower organizations to keep a vigilant eye on their risk landscape in real-time. Risk Heat Maps, for instance, offer a visual representation of risk data, allowing stakeholders to swiftly comprehend and respond to emerging patterns.

Technological innovations like Risk Management Information Systems (RMIS) streamline the monitoring process. These systems centralize risk-related information, facilitating easy access and analysis. Additionally, Key Risk Indicators (KRIs) serve as navigational beacons, providing early warnings of potential risk triggers, enabling organizations to enact timely interventions.

5.2.4 Integrated Risk Management Platforms

The pinnacle of contemporary risk management lies in Integrated Risk Management (IRM) platforms. These comprehensive solutions seamlessly integrate risk identification, assessment, and monitoring functions into a unified ecosystem. IRM platforms leverage automation, ensuring efficiency and accuracy in risk-related processes.

Equipped with robust reporting functionalities, IRM platforms furnish organizations with actionable insights. They enable cross-functional collaboration, breaking down silos and fostering a holistic approach to risk management.

At the core of their significance lies the ability to provide holistic oversight. Integrated Risk Management platforms act as the nerve center where risks from diverse business units and compliance facets converge. They offer a panoramic view, allowing organizations to grasp the interconnected nature of risks and align risk management strategies with the broader goals of governance and compliance within the GRC framework.

Centralization of data is a hallmark feature. These platforms serve as repositories, consolidating risk-related information into a single reservoir. This centralized data hub not only ensures real-time access but also guarantees that decision-makers possess accurate and current insights into the organization's risk landscape. Within GRC, where informed decision-making is pivotal, this unified data management becomes foundational.

Breaking down silos and fostering collaboration across functions is another forte of Integrated Risk Management platforms. By providing a shared space for assessing and managing risks, these platforms encourage communication and coordination among stakeholders from different corners of the organization. This collaborative ethos aligns seamlessly with the essence of GRC, where success hinges on cross-functional teamwork.

Automation takes center stage, streamlining the intricate dance of risk processes. Integrated Risk Management platforms automate key facets, from risk identification to assessment and monitoring. This not only reduces manual efforts but also ensures the consistent application of risk management protocols. In the dynamic GRC landscape, marked by the need for efficiency, automation becomes the engine that propels operational effectiveness.

Real-time monitoring of risks and robust reporting functionalities further elevate the stature of these platforms. They empower organizations with timely insights into emerging threats, enabling proactive responses. The ability to generate customized reports for stakeholders and regulatory bodies aligns with the reporting demands inherent in GRC, where transparency and accountability are non-negotiable.

5.3 Empowering Compliance Through Innovative Systems

In the intricate dance between businesses and regulatory frameworks, the implementation of Compliance Management Systems emerges as a linchpin for organizations striving not only to stay abreast of regulatory changes but also to seamlessly adhere to the ever-evolving landscape of compliance requirements. This chapter delves into the symbiotic relationship between technology and efficient compliance management, illuminating how innovative systems become the architects of organizational adherence and resilience.

Empowering compliance through innovative systems in Governance, Risk, and Compliance (GRC) encapsulates a transformative journey where technology emerges as the linchpin for effective and streamlined compliance processes. In this narrative, cutting-edge systems play a pivotal role in reshaping the compliance landscape, offering a spectrum of benefits that resonate within the broader GRC framework.

Automation becomes a cornerstone, as innovative systems seamlessly orchestrate compliance workflows, automating repetitive tasks and documentation processes. This not only reduces the likelihood of human error but liberates human resources for strategic endeavors, contributing to the efficiency and precision of compliance efforts within the dynamic GRC environment.

Real-time monitoring takes center stage, facilitated by advanced systems that continually scan for deviations from compliance standards. Automated alerts serve as vigilant sentinels, promptly notifying relevant stakeholders of potential issues and enabling swift corrective actions. This real-time responsiveness aligns with the proactive ethos required in GRC, ensuring that compliance risks are identified and addressed promptly.

The integration of Artificial Intelligence (AI) and analytics introduces a new dimension to compliance management. Innovative systems leverage AI to analyze vast datasets, unveiling patterns, trends, and potential risks. These insights, drawn from the data-rich GRC landscape, empower organizations to make informed, data-driven decisions and anticipate emerging compliance challenges.

Blockchain technology emerges as a safeguard for the integrity of compliance records. By creating tamper-proof ledgers, blockchain ensures the immutability and transparency of compliance-related transactions, providing a secure foundation for regulatory and internal audits. Trust and transparency, foundational principles in GRC, are fortified through the application of this innovative technology.

Cloud-based Compliance Management Systems offer a centralized hub accessible from anywhere, fostering collaboration and streamlining communication. In a globally connected GRC landscape, these systems enhance accessibility, enabling stakeholders to contribute to and access compliance information seamlessly. This adaptability contributes to a more agile and responsive compliance framework.

Robust cybersecurity measures, encompassing encryption and advanced authentication protocols, stand as guardians of sensitive compliance data. In an era where data protection is paramount, as data can also expose companies to risks if left undiscovered, unmonitored, and unprotected (The World Bank, 2023), these innovative systems ensure the confidentiality and integrity of compliance-related information, mitigating the risks associated with unauthorized access or breaches.

Continuous compliance monitoring, facilitated by dedicated tools, becomes a perpetual surveillance system. This ensures ongoing scrutiny of compliance activities, allowing organizations to promptly identify and rectify any deviations from established standards. This continuous monitoring aligns with the dynamic nature of GRC, providing organizations with the agility to adapt to changes in compliance requirements.

5.3.1 The Imperative of Compliance Management Systems

Navigating the labyrinth of regulations requires a strategic and systematic approach, and Compliance Management Systems stand at the forefront of this endeavor. At their core, these systems are the sentinels, tirelessly monitoring the regulatory horizon for changes, ensuring that organizations are not only aware of new mandates but are also well-equipped to integrate them seamlessly into their operational fabric. The imperative is not merely to comply but to do so with agility and foresight.

When it comes to Governance, Risk, and Compliance (GRC), the imperative of Compliance Management Systems (CMS) is akin to a steadfast guide steering organizations through the intricate paths of regulatory intricacies and ethical standards. Imagine a CMS as the organizational backbone, meticulously designed to ensure not just compliance with a plethora of regulations but a seamless integration of compliance into the broader GRC framework.

At its core, a CMS is the custodian of regulatory adherence. It acts as the organizational sentinel, ensuring that the entity operates within the legal confines and industry standards that govern its operations. In the expansive landscape of GRC, compliance isn't a mere checkbox; it's a foundational pillar. A robust CMS becomes the vanguard against legal repercussions and financial penalties, safeguarding the organization's integrity.

Beyond mere regulatory conformity, a well-integrated CMS plays a pivotal role in risk mitigation. It identifies, assesses, and addresses compliance risks, establishing controls and monitoring mechanisms that resonate throughout the GRC framework. In the dynamic dance of GRC, where risk management is intertwined with compliance, the CMS emerges as a linchpin in fortifying the organization's resilience against potential threats.

Operational efficiency, a cornerstone of GRC effectiveness, finds its ally in a streamlined CMS. By simplifying compliance processes and documentation, the CMS not only enhances day-to-day operations but also optimizes resource allocation. This efficiency doesn't merely check boxes; it aligns compliance activities with broader organizational goals, contributing to the overall efficacy of the GRC ecosystem.

Change is the only constant in the regulatory landscape, and a nimble CMS ensures organizations can gracefully adapt to these shifts. By efficiently tracking and updating compliance protocols, the CMS becomes the agile responder to regulatory changes, reducing the time lag between updates and implementation. In the interconnected nature of GRC, where agility is key, a responsive CMS is a strategic asset.

Comprehensive documentation and audit trails, inherent to a well-functioning CMS, lay the groundwork for transparency and accountability. GRC demands a clear understanding of compliance status and risk exposure. A robust CMS, by facilitating thorough documentation and auditing processes, becomes the storyteller that communicates the organization's commitment to governance and transparency.

The alignment of compliance efforts with an organization's values is not an afterthought but a deliberate endeavor fostered by an effective CMS. Beyond rules and regulations, compliance is about embodying the ethical essence of the organization. The CMS ensures that compliance activities harmonize with the ethical fabric of the organization, nurturing a culture of integrity and responsibility.

In the tapestry of GRC, proactive risk identification is a crucial thread, and the CMS excels in this role. By enabling the early identification of compliance issues, the CMS prevents them from evolving into substantial risks. This proactive stance aligns seamlessly with the GRC imperative of anticipating and addressing risks in their nascent stages.

5.3.2 Technological Integration in Compliance Management

The marriage of technology and compliance management heralds a new era of efficiency and accuracy. Organizations today leverage advanced technologies to streamline compliance processes, enhancing their ability to interpret, implement, and monitor regulatory requirements.

5.3.2.1 AUTOMATED COMPLIANCE TRACKING

Leading the charge is the integration of automated compliance tracking systems. These systems meticulously monitor regulatory changes, providing real-time updates and alerts. Through this automated vigilance, organizations can promptly assess the impact of new regulations on their operations and initiate responsive actions.

Also, automated compliance tracking represents a pivotal evolution in how organizations ensure adherence to regulatory standards, industry guidelines, and internal policies. This sophisticated process involves leveraging technology to automate the monitoring, assessment, and reporting of compliance activities, streamlining workflows and enhancing the overall effectiveness of an organization's compliance efforts.

I. **Real-Time Monitoring**

Automated compliance tracking introduces real-time monitoring capabilities. Instead of relying on periodic manual checks, organizations can deploy automated tools that continuously monitor activities against established compliance parameters. This real-time monitoring ensures a proactive response to any deviations or potential compliance issues.

II. **Comprehensive Data Aggregation**

Automated systems aggregate data from various sources relevant to compliance. These systems gather information from different departments, systems, and processes, creating a centralized repository of data. This aggregation ensures that compliance tracking encompasses the entirety of an organization's operations, providing a comprehensive view of its adherence to various standards.

III. **Rule-Based Compliance Checks:**

Automated compliance tracking operates on rule-based systems. Organizations can define specific rules, thresholds, and criteria for compliance within the automated tracking system. The technology then systematically checks activities against these predefined rules, instantly flagging any instances of non-compliance. This rule-based approach ensures consistency and accuracy in compliance evaluations.

IV. **Alerts and Notifications**

Automated systems generate alerts and notifications for non-compliance. When the system detects a deviation from established compliance parameters, it triggers alerts and notifications to relevant stakeholders. This immediate notification allows organizations to address non-compliance issues promptly, preventing potential risks and minimizing the impact on operations.

V. **Streamlined Reporting**

Automated compliance tracking simplifies the reporting process. Instead of manually compiling data for compliance reports, these systems generate streamlined, accurate, and up-to-date reports. This not only saves time but also provides management and regulatory authorities with a clear and transparent view of the organization's compliance status.

VI. **Auditable Trail**

Automated systems create an auditable trail of compliance activities. Every action, check, and decision related to compliance is recorded in an auditable trail. This trail serves as a historical record, facilitating internal audits and demonstrating to external regulators the organization's commitment to compliance.

VII. **Integration with Risk Management**

Automated compliance tracking integrates with overall risk management strategies. By connecting compliance tracking with risk management processes, organizations can assess the potential risks associated with non-compliance. This integrated approach ensures that compliance efforts align with broader risk mitigation strategies, contributing to a more holistic GRC framework.

VIII. **Continuous Improvement**

Automated compliance tracking supports continuous improvement initiatives. Analyzing data generated by the system allows organizations to identify patterns, trends, and areas for improvement. This data-driven insight empowers organizations to refine their compliance strategies, address recurring issues, and proactively enhance their overall compliance posture.

5.3.3 Regulatory Intelligence Platforms

Enter the era of Regulatory Intelligence Platforms, where data analytics and machine learning converge to offer organizations a deeper understanding of regulatory landscapes. These platforms sift through vast datasets, extracting insights that empower decision-makers to anticipate regulatory trends and proactively shape compliance strategies.

Also, Regulatory Intelligence Platforms emerge as advanced navigators, akin to wise guides in a constantly shifting landscape. Picture a sophisticated system that not only gathers information but interprets and disseminates regulatory nuances, acting as a guiding light for organizations seeking to navigate the complexities of compliance seamlessly.

These platforms act as meticulous architects, gathering vast amounts of regulatory data from diverse sources. They function as vigilant sentinels, ensuring organizations stay abreast of changes in regulations emanating from regulatory bodies, industry publications, and government updates.

Yet, their prowess extends beyond mere data collection. Regulatory Intelligence Platforms serve as interpreters, unraveling the intricate language of regulations and providing insightful analyses. They become translators of complexity, offering organizations a clear understanding of how regulatory changes might impact their compliance status and overall business operations.

A defining feature lies in their ability to provide customized alerts and notifications. Tailored to an organization's specific regulatory landscape, these platforms push real-time notifications, ensuring prompt awareness of any regulatory developments demanding attention or action.

Imagine these platforms as architects of regulatory landscapes, crafting maps and compliance roadmaps for organizations. They outline the regulatory terrain relevant to an industry, guiding organizations on the necessary steps to ensure adherence to existing and upcoming regulatory requirements.

Facilitating collaboration is another integral aspect. Regulatory Intelligence Platforms provide centralized communication channels, ensuring that relevant stakeholders within the organization can discuss, strategize, and implement necessary changes in response to regulatory updates.

Seamless integration with risk assessment processes enhances their utility. By linking regulatory intelligence with risk assessments, organizations can assess the potential impact of regulatory changes on their risk profile. This integration fosters a holistic approach, allowing organizations to align compliance efforts with broader risk management strategies.

Maintaining historical data and an auditable trail, these platforms create invaluable resources for internal audits. They showcase how an organization has navigated regulatory changes over time, providing a comprehensive record of compliance landscapes.

Designed for continuous learning and adaptation, Regulatory Intelligence Platforms evolve with the regulatory landscape. They learn from past trends, adapt to emerging patterns, and ensure that organizations stay ahead of the curve. This commitment to continuous learning enables organizations to proactively adjust their compliance strategies in anticipation of future regulatory developments.

5.3.4 Streamlining Compliance Processes

Compliance management is not merely about reacting to changes; it's about instilling a proactive ethos within organizational DNA. Technology plays a pivotal role in streamlining compliance processes, ensuring they are not only effective but also efficient.

5.3.4.1 DOCUMENT MANAGEMENT SYSTEMS

Organizations harness Document Management Systems (DMS) to centralize and organize compliance-related documentation. This not only fosters accessibility but also ensures that the right stakeholders have real-time access to the latest versions of policies, procedures, and regulatory guidelines.

Furthermore, DMS emerge as indispensable architects, reshaping the landscape of compliance processes. Picture a sophisticated system that transcends conventional document storage, offering a comprehensive suite of functionalities meticulously designed to organize, track, and safeguard critical documents, all while harmonizing seamlessly with compliance objectives.

At the heart of this system lies a centralized repository, a digital fortress that consolidates all compliance-related documents. No longer scattered across disparate platforms, these documents find a unified home, fostering easy access and efficient management. Moreover, DMS introduces the concept of version control and an audit trail, ensuring that the most current iterations are easily identifiable, while an audit trail provides a transparent historical record of document changes.

Security is paramount, and DMS rises to the occasion with robust features such as encryption and access controls. Sensitive compliance documents are shielded, and access permissions can be finely tuned, allowing only authorized personnel to delve into the intricacies of these documents.

Workflow automation becomes the virtuoso, orchestrating document approvals and reviews with precision. This systematic approach minimizes the risk of oversight, ensuring that compliance documents undergo the necessary checks in a timely manner. Collaboration takes center stage as DMS facilitates real-time collaboration and remote access. Teams, regardless of their geographical locations, can seamlessly contribute to compliance documents, fostering collaboration among stakeholders and accommodating the demands of remote work scenarios.

The organizational symphony continues with document tagging and categorization, simplifying the organization and retrieval of compliance documents. Automation extends to document retention policies, ensuring adherence to legal and regulatory requirements regarding document retention and disposal.

Integration is a key theme as DMS seamlessly merges with Compliance Management Systems, creating a symbiotic relationship. Changes or updates in compliance requirements are effortlessly reflected in the documents, creating a cohesive environment that aligns compliance documents with broader compliance initiatives.

Advanced search and retrieval capabilities enhance the agility of compliance processes. Users can swiftly locate specific compliance documents using keywords or metadata, reducing the time spent on manual searches and contributing to operational efficiency. Reporting and analytics become the concluding notes in this symphony, allowing organizations to generate insightful reports on document-related metrics, track document status, and analyze trends. This data-driven approach aids in assessing the efficiency of compliance processes and identifying areas for improvement.

In essence, Document Management Systems, in the context of compliance processes, stand as vigilant custodians, bringing order, security, and efficiency to the forefront. By centralizing documents, ensuring version control, implementing security measures, automating workflows, facilitating collaboration, and seamlessly integrating with broader compliance initiatives, DMS transforms compliance documentation into a well-orchestrated symphony of organized, secure, and easily accessible information. It becomes an indispensable tool in the GRC arsenal, contributing significantly to the organization's overall governance and risk management objectives.

5.3.4.2 WORKFLOW AUTOMATION

The orchestration of compliance workflows is revolutionized through automation. Workflow automation tools enable organizations to design, implement, and monitor compliance processes with precision. This not only reduces the margin for error but also expedites response times to regulatory changes.

Picture a digital conductor guiding the intricate steps of governance, risk management, and compliance through seamlessly automated workflows, navigating the complex terrain of regulatory landscapes with precision.

In the realm of risk assessment and mitigation, workflow automation takes the lead, streamlining processes from identification to mitigation. By following predefined paths, it minimizes oversights and ensures a proactive approach to managing risks.

Compliance monitoring and reporting find a reliable ally in automated workflows. These workflows track compliance requirements in real-time, providing organizations with the agility to respond to evolving regulatory standards promptly.

Incident response and resolution become a well-choreographed routine as automated workflows establish predefined paths for addressing incidents. This ensures a swift and organized approach to resolving issues while adhering to regulatory reporting requirements.

For policy management and documentation, workflow automation ensures a seamless lifecycle. From creation and review to dissemination, workflows adhere to established protocols, minimizing manual interventions and ensuring policy adherence.

Maintaining an audit trail and documentation of GRC activities is a forte of workflow automation. By recording each step in GRC processes, it creates a transparent audit trail, ensuring compliance with regulatory requirements and facilitating internal and external audits.

Cross-functional collaboration is promoted as workflow automation extends its reach to multiple departments involved in GRC, fostering collaboration and breaking down silos. This ensures a holistic approach to GRC, aligning various functions toward common objectives.

In the face of regulatory changes, automated workflows showcase their adaptability. They guide organizations through the process of updating policies, conducting risk assessments, and ensuring that stakeholders are informed and aligned, contributing to change management in GRC.

Continuous monitoring and improvement become ingrained in GRC processes through workflow automation. By constantly monitoring activities, organizations identify areas for enhancement, ensuring that processes evolve to meet changing regulatory landscapes and internal requirements.

Documented evidence for compliance activities is a hallmark of automated workflows. By automatically documenting each step in the GRC process, workflows create a repository of evidence crucial for demonstrating compliance during audits or regulatory inquiries.

Real-time notifications and alerts are woven into the fabric of workflow automation in GRC. Automated notifications keep stakeholders informed about the status of GRC processes, upcoming deadlines, and actions that require attention, enabling proactive decision-making and timely interventions.

In essence, workflow automation in GRC is the virtuoso conductor orchestrating a seamless integration of governance, risk management, and compliance processes. By automating routine tasks, ensuring compliance, fostering collaboration, and supporting adaptability, workflow automation becomes an invaluable asset in navigating the intricate landscape of GRC with precision and agility.

5.4 Proactive Compliance Culture

Beyond the technological infrastructure, fostering a proactive compliance culture is paramount. Compliance Management Systems serve as catalysts in this cultural evolution, acting as enablers rather than constraints.

Cultivating a proactive compliance culture in the dynamic realm of Governance, Risk, and Compliance (GRC) involves instilling a mindset where compliance transcends a set of regulations to become an intrinsic element of an organization's identity. In this narrative, the proactive compliance culture unfolds as a strategic imperative, woven into the organizational fabric through a series of cultural catalysts.

At the forefront, leadership emerges as the torchbearer of this cultural shift. Leaders set the tone by not just endorsing compliance but championing it as a strategic cornerstone. Their advocacy transforms compliance from a mandatory requirement into a vital component aligning with organizational goals.

Communication and training serve as pivotal elements, nurturing comprehension and commitment. Transparent communication about compliance expectations, coupled with training programs, ensures that employees grasp not only the rules but also the rationale behind them. This approach fosters a culture where compliance is understood, valued, and willingly adhered to.

The integration of compliance into everyday processes becomes a cultural catalyst, dispelling the notion of compliance as an extraneous burden. Automation reinforces this integration, with compliance checks seamlessly embedded into workflows. As a result, compliance becomes a natural and intuitive part of the organizational routine.

Proactivity thrives on data-driven insights. Organizations leverage analytics and reporting tools to gain real-time visibility into compliance metrics. This approach transforms compliance from a reactive task to a proactive endeavor, allowing for the anticipation and mitigation of potential issues before they escalate.

Empowering employees as compliance advocates forms a decentralized network of vigilant contributors. By providing knowledge and tools, organizations turn every employee into a stakeholder, fostering a culture where compliance risks are identified and addressed at various levels of the organization.

Continuous monitoring and auditing contribute to ongoing vigilance. Rather than viewing audits as mere checkpoints, they become opportunities for learning and improvement. This continuous evaluation identifies and rectifies compliance issues proactively, preventing them from becoming systemic.

Recognition and incentives serve as positive reinforcement, acknowledging and rewarding compliance achievements. This recognition motivates employees and teams to actively contribute to the compliance culture, creating a positive feedback loop.

A proactive compliance culture embraces a learning mindset, acknowledging the dynamic nature of compliance landscapes. Organizations encourage continuous learning, staying informed about regulatory changes, and proactively adjusting their compliance strategies.

Collaboration across departments is crucial. A proactive compliance culture fosters open communication and collaboration, recognizing that compliance is a collaborative effort that transcends individual departments.

Lastly, accountability and consequences uphold responsibility. Clearly defined expectations and consequences for non-compliance create a sense of accountability. This awareness motivates individuals to proactively adhere to established standards.

5.5 NAVIGATING THE GRC TAPESTRY IN DYNAMIC ENVIRONMENTS

In the fluid expanse of contemporary business, the Governance, Risk, and Compliance (GRC) landscape weave a tapestry that continually evolves. Successful navigation through this intricate web demands not just adherence to established principles but also a keen adaptability to the dynamic currents of the business environment. This chapter unfolds strategies, akin to a compass, guiding organizations in anticipating and effectively addressing changes in governance, risk, and compliance.

5.5.1 THE DYNAMIC CANVAS OF GRC

The foundation of GRC is laid upon a dynamic canvas, where the elements of governance, risk, and compliance are not static pillars but rather fluid entities subject to constant change. Recognizing this inherent dynamism is the first step in crafting a strategy that transcends rigidity.

At the heart of this dynamic landscape is the ever-evolving regulatory environment, a canvas where the rules are not static but subject to constant flux. Organizations find themselves in a perpetual dance, keeping pace with new laws, amendments, and global shifts that demand agility and responsiveness. The brushstrokes of technology paint a rapidly progressing scene, with innovations like artificial intelligence and blockchain reshaping how governance, risk, and compliance are managed.

Globalization adds complexity to the canvas, intertwining networks and presenting diverse regulatory landscapes and cultural nuances. The canvas is marked by a deluge of data and the persistent specter of cybersecurity threats, demanding constant vigilance and adaptive strategies. Stakeholder expectations form dynamic hues, influenced by societal changes, ethical considerations, and environmental concerns, shaping the narrative of corporate responsibility.

The canvas is characterized by interconnected risks, recognizing that disruptions in one area can reverberate throughout the entire ecosystem. Organizational dynamics contribute to the tableau, with cultural shifts and changes in leadership influencing how governance is implemented, risks are assessed, and compliance is maintained. Social and environmental considerations are integral, adding evolving dimensions that organizations must incorporate to align with societal expectations.

Economic variability introduces market dynamics that create undulating patterns on the canvas. Organizations must navigate economic fluctuations and unforeseen market shifts that impact governance, introduce new risks, or necessitate adjustments in compliance strategies. In this ever-shifting landscape, a continuous improvement mandate becomes the guiding principle, urging organizations to embrace a culture of learning, assess the effectiveness of GRC strategies, and proactively enhance their frameworks.

5.5.2 Proactive Risk Anticipation

Risk, an ever-present companion in the business journey, demands a proactive stance in dynamic environments. Strategies for risk anticipation become the sentinel, standing guard against potential disruptions.

In the realm of Governance, Risk, and Compliance (GRC), proactive risk anticipation unfolds as a strategic art form, where organizations endeavor to decipher the subtle nuances of potential risks before they manifest into formidable challenges. This anticipatory mindset, akin to a vigilant sentinel, is a cornerstone of effective risk management within the dynamic business landscape.

At the genesis of proactive risk anticipation lies a meticulous process of risk identification. Organizations embark on a holistic journey, scrutinizing internal and external factors that could cast shadows on their objectives. This encompasses a thorough examination of emerging trends, market dynamics, technological shifts, and the ever-changing regulatory landscape.

A key brushstroke in this anticipatory canvas is scenario planning. Organizations engage in the art of crafting hypothetical situations, projecting the potential unfoldings of various risks. This forward-looking approach serves as a strategic compass, enabling a deeper understanding of vulnerabilities and facilitating the formulation of preemptive strategies.

The palette of proactive risk anticipation is enriched with the hues of data analytics and predictive modeling. By harnessing the power of data, organizations glean insights from historical patterns and trends, laying the groundwork for foreseeing potential risk scenarios. Continuous monitoring, akin to a vigilant guardian, becomes a pivotal element, with real-time systems detecting early warning signs and paving the way for timely intervention.

Stakeholder engagement adds a collaborative dimension to the canvas. Internal and external voices, ranging from employees to industry experts, contribute unique perspectives, enriching the organization's ability to anticipate risks that may be concealed in the intricate tapestry of operations.

Navigating the regulatory landscape with an astute eye is another stroke in this masterpiece. Proactive organizations remain attuned to regulatory changes, interpreting and adapting to evolving compliance requirements with agility and foresight.

Technology emerges as a transformative force in the brushstrokes of risk anticipation. The integration of artificial intelligence and machine learning technologies empowers organizations to analyze vast datasets, discern patterns, and glean predictive insights, equipping them with a proactive edge.

Cross-functional collaboration becomes the harmonious blending of colors, breaking down silos and fostering a collaborative ethos. This integrated approach ensures a holistic understanding of risks that may transcend departmental boundaries.

Training and awareness programs act as a nurturing force, cultivating a culture of risk vigilance among employees. An educated and informed workforce becomes a collective eye, adept at spotting early indicators of risks and proactively contributing to the risk management ecosystem.

Finally, assessing risk tolerance aligns the strategic vision with the brushstrokes of risk anticipation. Understanding and aligning risk management strategies with the organization's risk appetite and overarching objectives ensures a proactive approach that resonates with the organization's risk tolerance.

5.5.3 Adaptive Compliance Strategies

Compliance, a stalwart companion in the GRC triad, necessitates adaptive strategies in the face of evolving regulations and standards.

In the intricate tapestry of Governance, Risk, and Compliance (GRC), adaptive compliance strategies emerge as a dynamic and responsive brushstroke. Organizations, recognizing the fluidity of regulatory landscapes, embrace a strategy that is not merely reactive but anticipatory and flexible.

At the core of adaptive compliance is the commitment to real-time regulatory intelligence. Organizations establish vigilant monitoring systems, ensuring that any alterations in regulatory requirements are promptly detected and seamlessly integrated into the compliance fabric. This continuous awareness becomes the cornerstone of an agile response to evolving compliance demands.

Flexibility and scalability characterize adaptive compliance. Organizations craft compliance frameworks that can be tailored to suit the nuances of specific regulatory contexts. This adaptability allows for the fluid adjustment of compliance processes, ensuring alignment with the ever-changing regulatory landscape.

Technology, a transformative force in this narrative, integrates seamlessly into adaptive compliance. Automation becomes the silent orchestrator, streamlining compliance processes and enhancing operational efficiency. Analytics tools provide organizations with actionable insights, empowering them to proactively address potential compliance challenges before they escalate.

Cross-functional collaboration is the harmony that resonates in adaptive compliance. Breaking down departmental silos ensures that compliance efforts are holistic, with various functions working in concert. This collaborative ethos not only enhances the effectiveness of compliance but also fosters a shared understanding of regulatory obligations.

A risk-based approach becomes the guiding principle in adaptive compliance. Organizations conduct thorough risk assessments to identify areas of higher regulatory impact. This enables strategic resource allocation, directing efforts towards mitigating risks that carry the most significant compliance implications.

Continuous training and awareness initiatives weave a thread of empowerment. Informed employees become frontline contributors to compliance efforts, and a culture of compliance consciousness permeates the organizational fabric.

Scenario planning and contingency measures form a shield against unforeseen regulatory shifts. Organizations, in an anticipatory stance, craft strategic responses to potential regulatory scenarios, ensuring they are well-prepared for any unexpected changes.

Proactive engagement with regulatory bodies becomes a proactive dialogue. Organizations establish open channels of communication, advocating for clarity in regulatory expectations. This collaborative approach enables organizations to navigate compliance requirements more effectively.

Continuous improvement and feedback loops form the iterative heartbeat of adaptive compliance. Organizations regularly assess the effectiveness of their compliance strategies, incorporating lessons learned and refining their frameworks to remain responsive and resilient.

Cultural integration completes the portrait of adaptive compliance. It goes beyond processes, embedding a compliance culture within the organizational DNA. Employees embrace compliance as a collective responsibility, and the organizational culture aligns seamlessly with the principles of governance and risk management.

5.5.4 Technology as an Enabler

In the toolkit for navigating dynamic GRC landscapes, technology emerges as a potent enabler.

Technology acts as an efficiency amplifier, automating repetitive GRC tasks. This not only reduces the risk of errors but also allows organizations to allocate resources strategically, focusing on more nuanced aspects of governance, risk management, and compliance.

Data analytics and predictive insights become the guiding stars in this technological journey. Organizations harness the power of technology to analyze vast datasets, uncovering patterns, trends, and potential risks. This data-driven approach equips decision-makers with the knowledge needed for informed and strategic decision-making in the realms of governance and risk management.

Integrated risk management platforms, a testament to technological prowess, provide a panoramic view of risks. By consolidating information from various sources, technology breaks down silos, fostering a unified approach to risk management. This holistic perspective enables organizations to assess and manage risks comprehensively, ensuring a robust defense against potential threats.

In the realm of compliance, technology acts as a beacon of proactivity through regulatory intelligence platforms. Real-time monitoring of regulatory changes ensures that organizations receive timely updates on evolving compliance requirements. This real-time vigilance allows for swift adaptation and proactive adherence to the latest regulations.

Document management systems, powered by technology, streamline compliance documentation. By organizing and centralizing compliance-related documents, organizations not only ensure efficient documentation but also simplify audit processes, enhancing the overall compliance posture.

Workflow automation, a symphony of technology and streamlined processes, ensures that GRC tasks follow predefined sequences. This reduces manual intervention, leading to more efficient workflows in tasks such as risk assessments, policy management, and compliance monitoring.

Artificial Intelligence (AI) and Machine Learning (ML) technologies contribute to predictive risk modeling. By analyzing historical data, these technologies predict potential risks and trends, enabling organizations to proactively address emerging threats before they escalate.

Continuous monitoring and alerts, facilitated by technology, provide real-time vigilance over key risk indicators and compliance metrics. Automated alerts notify stakeholders of deviations or potential issues, allowing for immediate intervention and mitigation.

Mobile applications become the gateway to accessible GRC. Stakeholders gain on-the-go access to critical GRC information, enhancing communication, collaboration, and decision-making in dynamic environments where quick responses are essential.

Blockchain technology, a technological marvel, enhances security and transparency in GRC processes. Providing an immutable and decentralized ledger, blockchain ensures the integrity of critical governance and compliance information, fostering trust in the digital era.

5.5.5 Cultivating a Dynamic GRC Culture

Beyond structures and strategies, cultivating a dynamic GRC culture is paramount. This involves instilling a mindset that embraces change as an opportunity rather than a threat.

5.6 Continuous Learning and Training

In a dynamic GRC environment, knowledge is a dynamic currency. Continuous learning and training initiatives ensure that stakeholders are equipped with the skills needed to navigate evolving landscapes. This includes staying abreast of new regulations, refining risk management techniques, and adapting governance structures.

Within this culture, the concept of lifelong learning takes center stage. It instills in employees a mindset of perpetual curiosity and adaptability, preparing them to navigate seamlessly through the dynamic shifts in governance structures, emerging risks, and the ever-evolving landscape of compliance requirements.

Regular training programs become the artisans molding the skill set of individuals. These programs, thoughtfully designed to address specific GRC competencies, serve as crucibles for refining capabilities in areas such as risk assessment methodologies, compliance frameworks, and governance best practices.

As technology assumes a pivotal role in modern GRC practices, ongoing training becomes the compass guiding employees through the intricate terrain of technological tools. Proficiency in GRC software, data analytics tools, and other technological solutions becomes not just a skill but a strategic asset.

The flux of regulations demands continuous vigilance, prompting organizations to conduct workshops and training sessions focused on interpreting and implementing new regulatory standards.

Staying informed about the evolving regulatory landscape becomes a collective effort woven into the fabric of the organization.

Cross-functional knowledge sharing becomes the collaborative symphony in this learning culture. As individuals from different departments contribute insights and experiences, a holistic understanding of GRC challenges and solutions emerges, enriching the collective intelligence of the organization.

Scenario-based training becomes the canvas where theoretical knowledge meets practical application. These simulations provide employees with the opportunity to hone their decision-making skills, practice risk management techniques, and develop effective compliance strategies in a controlled and supportive environment.

Certification programs, akin to badges of honor, formally recognize expertise in GRC. Individuals completing these programs not only demonstrate a commitment to continuous learning but also signify mastery of specific GRC competencies, contributing tangible value to both the individual and the organization.

GRC learning portals become the repositories of self-directed learning, offering resources, modules, and case studies that employees can explore at their own pace. This autonomy encourages a proactive approach to skill development, allowing individuals to tailor their learning journey to their specific needs.

Continuous learning extends beyond the technicalities to encompass compliance training on ethical standards. This facet ensures that employees not only comprehend the regulatory landscape but also adhere to ethical principles, fostering a culture of integrity, responsibility, and ethical conduct.

Feedback and improvement loops complete the iterative cycle of continuous learning. Regular assessments and feedback mechanisms enable organizations to identify areas for enhancement in their training programs, ensuring they remain relevant, effective, and finely tuned to the evolving demands of GRC.

CHAPTER SIX

SUSTAINING EXCELLENCE: CONTINUOUS MONITORING AND IMPROVEMENT IN THE GRC ODYSSEY

Within the Governance, Risk, and Compliance (GRC) journey, the only constant is change. This chapter illuminates the critical significance of continuous monitoring and improvement, underscoring the dynamic nature of the GRC process. As organizations navigate the ever-shifting landscape, the implementation of feedback loops, meticulous tracking of key performance indicators (KPIs), and regular assessments emerge as the compass guiding the perpetual pursuit of excellence.

6.1 The Dynamic Essence of Continuous Monitoring and Improvement

The essence of GRC lies not in achieving a static state of perfection but in the perpetual journey towards excellence. Continuous monitoring and improvement serve as the lifeblood of this journey, acknowledging that the GRC landscape is an evolving tapestry that demands vigilant attention and responsive action.

Continuous monitoring acts as a vigilant sentinel, operating in real-time to provide organizations with a dynamic awareness of key risk indicators, compliance metrics, and governance processes. It ensures that potential issues are identified promptly, allowing for swift intervention and mitigation.

Feedback loops become the heartbeat of this iterative improvement process. Regular assessments and feedback mechanisms create a continuous cycle where insights from monitoring efforts contribute to refining strategies, policies, and processes. This constant loop of evaluation and adjustment ensures that the organization is responsive to changing dynamics.

Key Performance Indicators (KPIs) serve as the compass guiding continuous monitoring efforts. These metrics, aligned with organizational objectives, enable the quantification of GRC effectiveness. Regular evaluation against KPIs serves as a barometer for success and areas needing improvement, driving a culture of measurable success.

The proactive nature of continuous monitoring extends to risk mitigation, allowing organizations to anticipate potential challenges rather than adopting a reactive stance. This preemptive approach reduces the likelihood and impact of adverse events on governance, risk management, and compliance.

Adaptive governance structures emerge as a necessity in this dynamic environment. Continuous monitoring facilitates an approach where governance structures evolve in response to changing circumstances. This adaptability ensures that governance remains effective and aligned with organizational goals.

Dynamic compliance strategies are a natural outcome of continuous monitoring. Compliance requirements are not static, and this approach ensures that strategies evolve alongside regulatory changes. Organizations can stay ahead of compliance curves, mitigating the risk of non-compliance through proactive adjustments.

Regular assessments, integral to continuous monitoring, provide a holistic evaluation of the entire GRC framework. This includes assessing the effectiveness of risk management processes, the robustness of compliance measures, and the efficiency of governance structures. The insights gained drive targeted improvements.

Flexibility in risk management is a hallmark of continuous monitoring. It allows organizations to adjust risk mitigation strategies swiftly in response to emerging threats or changes in the business landscape. This agility ensures a resilient risk management framework that can adapt to evolving challenges.

The dynamic essence of continuous monitoring cultivates a learning culture within the organization. It fosters a mindset of adaptability and a commitment to learning from monitoring outcomes. Challenges are seen as opportunities for improvement, and the organization becomes adept at transforming setbacks into stepping stones for progress.

The integration of technology plays a crucial role in making continuous monitoring efficient and effective. Automated tools and systems enhance the speed and accuracy of data collection, analysis, and reporting, enabling a seamless and real-time monitoring process that aligns with the pace of a dynamic GRC landscape.

Adaptive Feedback Loops: At the heart of continuous improvement lies the incorporation of adaptive feedback loops. These loops act as conduits for insights, allowing organizations to gather real-time feedback from stakeholders, internal processes, and external environments. By fostering a culture that embraces feedback, organizations create a dynamic ecosystem where lessons learned today fuel improvements tomorrow.

6.2 The Guiding Beacons - Key Performance Indicators (KPIs)

In the quest for excellence, organizations must rely on guiding beacons to measure and track their progress. Key Performance Indicators (KPIs) stand as essential metrics, offering insights into the effectiveness of governance structures, risk management frameworks, and compliance strategies.

Strategic KPIs for Governance: For governance, strategic KPIs might include the efficacy of decision-making processes, the responsiveness of governance committees, and the alignment of governance structures with organizational objectives. These indicators serve as compass points, ensuring that governance remains not just a procedural formality but a dynamic force steering the organization towards its goals.

Risk-Infused KPIs: In the realm of risk management, KPIs are imbued with the power to quantify and qualify an organization's resilience. Metrics such as risk appetite adherence, the effectiveness of risk mitigation strategies, and the speed of response to emerging risks become the barometers of risk maturity. Continuous monitoring of these KPIs enables organizations to not only weather storms but to navigate them with finesse.

Compliance Metrics as Benchmarks: Compliance, too, finds its benchmarks in KPIs. Metrics measuring the rate of compliance with regulations, the efficiency of compliance processes, and the level of stakeholder trust become the litmus test for organizational integrity. Regular monitoring of compliance KPIs ensures that organizations not only meet current standards but proactively shape future compliance strategies.

6.3 The Rhythm of Regular Assessments

In the orchestra of GRC, regular assessments are the harmonious notes that validate the efficacy of strategies and processes.

These assessments serve as the strategic moments when the organization takes stock of its GRC landscape, fine-tuning its strategies and ensuring that every note aligns harmoniously with the overarching objectives. The regularity of these assessments is not merely a ritual but a deliberate and strategic choice, woven into the fabric of a proactive GRC culture.

I. Holistic Evaluation

Comprehensive Insight: Regular assessments in GRC are akin to a conductor's baton guiding a comprehensive evaluation of the entire governance, risk management, and compliance framework. This holistic approach ensures that every facet of the organization's GRC landscape is scrutinized.

II. Key Performance Indicators (KPIs)

Measuring Success: The rhythm of regular assessments is synchronized with the beat of Key Performance Indicators (KPIs). These metrics, carefully chosen to align with organizational objectives, provide a quantitative measure of GRC success, guiding the organization towards its strategic goals.

III. Iterative Refinement

Continuous Improvement: Like a recurring musical motif, regular assessments create an environment of continuous improvement. Insights gleaned from assessments become the sheet music for refining strategies, policies, and procedures, ensuring that the organization evolves in tune with emerging challenges.

IV. Responsive Risk Mitigation

Adapting to Dynamics: In the ever-shifting landscape of risks, regular assessments provide the rhythm for responsive risk mitigation. Organizations can adjust their risk management strategies based on current assessments, ensuring that they are attuned to the dynamic nature of emerging threats.

V. Compliance Alignment

Ensuring Adherence: Compliance requirements are not static, and the regular beat of assessments ensures that the organization's compliance measures are in tune with evolving regulatory landscapes. This alignment safeguards against the discord of non-compliance.

VI. **Continuous Learning Culture**

Harvesting Insights: Regular assessments foster a culture of continuous learning. Each assessment becomes a lesson, and the insights gained contribute to the collective intelligence of the organization, creating a culture where mistakes are viewed as opportunities for refinement.

VII. **Scenario-Based Evaluations**

Real-world Simulations: Just as a musician practices with different scenarios, GRC assessments often involve scenario-based evaluations. These simulations provide a practical context for testing the organization's response to various GRC challenges, ensuring preparedness for real-world scenarios.

VIII. **Transparent Communication**

Open Dialogue: The rhythm of regular assessments is accompanied by a melody of transparent communication. Stakeholders are engaged in an open dialogue about the assessment findings, ensuring that everyone is attuned to the organization's GRC performance and areas for improvement.

IX. **Strategic Decision-Making**

Informed Choices: Regular assessments provide the necessary notes for strategic decision-making. Leaders can make informed choices based on the current state of GRC, guiding the organization's direction with a clarity that comes from the regular evaluation of its GRC initiatives.

X. **Adaptability to Change**

Flexibility in Tune: The rhythm of regular assessments instills adaptability. Organizations become nimble, capable of adjusting their GRC strategies in response to changing internal and external dynamics, ensuring that the tune remains harmonious in the face of uncertainties.

6.4 The Ongoing Evolution - A Dynamic GRC Culture

Continuous monitoring and improvement are not just procedural elements but integral components of an organizational culture that thrives on evolution.

In the intricate fabric of Governance, Risk, and Compliance (GRC), the ongoing evolution signifies the cultivation of a dynamic GRC culture, a living entity that adapts, learns, and thrives in the face of continuous change. This dynamic culture is not a static set of principles but a fluid and responsive approach that embraces evolution as an inherent aspect of its existence.

I. **Continuous Learning and Adaptation**

Ingrained Learning: A dynamic GRC culture is characterized by an ingrained commitment to continuous learning. It thrives on acquiring new knowledge, understanding emerging risks, and adapting strategies to navigate an ever-changing landscape.

II. **Proactive Risk Anticipation**

Anticipating Challenges: Instead of merely reacting to challenges, a dynamic GRC culture proactively anticipates risks. It fosters a mindset where potential threats are identified early, allowing for strategic planning and mitigation strategies before issues escalate.

III. **Agility in Governance**

Responsive Governance Structures: Traditional governance structures may be rigid, but a dynamic GRC culture embraces agility. It recognizes the need for governance structures that can flex and adapt to changing circumstances, ensuring relevance and effectiveness.

IV. **Adaptable Compliance Strategies**

Evolving Compliance Practices: Compliance is not a static checkbox; it's a dynamic process. A dynamic GRC culture ensures that compliance strategies are adaptable, evolving alongside regulatory changes to maintain a proactive and responsive stance.

V. **Technology Integration**

Harnessing Technological Advances: Embracing technological advancements is integral to a dynamic GRC culture. This involves the strategic integration of cutting-edge technologies to enhance efficiency, automate processes, and stay ahead in a technologically evolving landscape.

VI. **Collaborative Decision-Making**

Collective Intelligence: Instead of siloed decision-making, a dynamic GRC culture encourages collaborative approaches. It leverages the collective intelligence of diverse teams, fostering a culture where insights from different perspectives contribute to more robust decision-making.

VII. **Continuous Improvement Mindset**

Iterative Refinement: Continuous improvement is not a sporadic event but a continuous process. A dynamic GRC culture nurtures a mindset where every aspect of governance, risk management, and compliance is subject to iterative refinement based on ongoing assessments and feedback.

VIII. Resilience in the Face of Setbacks

Adapting to Setbacks: Challenges and setbacks are inevitable, but a dynamic GRC culture views them as opportunities for adaptation and growth. It embraces resilience, bouncing back from setbacks with newfound insights and fortified strategies.

IX. Transparent Communication

Open Dialogue: Transparent communication is the lifeblood of a dynamic GRC culture. It ensures that information flows seamlessly across departments, fostering an environment where stakeholders are well-informed, contributing to a shared understanding of GRC goals.

X. Strategic Alignment with Business Goals

Integration with Business Strategy: A dynamic GRC culture aligns with broader business goals. It integrates GRC practices into the overall business strategy, recognizing that effective governance and risk management are integral components of sustainable business success.

CHAPTER SEVEN

CASE STUDIES AND BEST PRACTICES

This chapter explores the best practices and generic examples of Governance, Risk and Compliance (GRC). For an individual with a non-tech background, going over case-studies is one of the surest ways to familiarize oneself with how GRC professionals make important decisions.

It offers an insight into different premises of the issues, experts have to deal with to ensure that there are no costly breaches. Be it real-life case studies or simulations, every form of learning you acquire at this point is vital because "transitioning into cybersecurity GRC requires patience and persistence. While you might not have an IT background, your dedication to learning, combined with practical experience and continuous growth, will be crucial in building a successful career in this field." (Abdullah Mahjoub 2023).

Here are the outlines of some generic examples and best practices in Governance, Risk, and Compliance (GRC).

Case Study 1: Cybersecurity Governance

BACKGROUND

A multinational financial institution implemented a robust cybersecurity governance framework to protect sensitive customer information and uphold regulatory compliance.

BEST PRACTICES

1. Board Involvement: The board was actively involved in setting cybersecurity governance policies and regularly reviewed and approved cybersecurity strategies.

2. Risk Assessment: The organization conducted regular risk assessments to identify vulnerabilities and threats, ensuring a proactive approach to cybersecurity.

3. Compliance Adherence: The cybersecurity governance framework aligned with international cybersecurity standards, and the organization regularly updated its policies to comply with emerging regulations.

4. Incident Response Plan: A comprehensive incident response plan was in place, detailing the steps to be taken in case of a cybersecurity breach. Regular drills were conducted to test the effectiveness of the plan.

Case Study 2: Enterprise Risk Management (ERM) in Manufacturing

Background:

A manufacturing company implemented an ERM system to address risks associated with supply chain disruptions, market fluctuations, and regulatory changes.

Best Practices:

1. Integrated Risk Culture: The company fostered a risk-aware culture where employees at all levels were encouraged to identify and report risks. This ensured a holistic approach to risk management.

2. Supply Chain Visibility: The ERM system incorporated real-time monitoring of the supply chain, allowing the company to identify potential disruptions and implement contingency plans swiftly.

3. Continuous Monitoring: The organization employed data analytics to continuously monitor key risk indicators, enabling proactive risk mitigation strategies.

4. Stakeholder Engagement: Regular communication with suppliers, regulators, and other stakeholders helped the company stay informed about external factors influencing risk and compliance.

BEST PRACTICES IN GRC

1. **Integrated GRC Platforms:**

   Scenario Planning: Use integrated GRC platforms that facilitate scenario planning for anticipating and addressing emerging risks.

2. **Dynamic Policy Management:**

   Regular Updates: Adopt dynamic policy management systems that allow for real-time updates, ensuring policies remain aligned with regulatory changes.

3. **Data-Driven Decision-Making:**

   Business Intelligence: Utilize data-driven decision-making processes to gather insights for informed, agile decision-making in response to dynamic changes.

4. **Continuous Learning and Training:**

   Training Programs: Implement continuous learning and training programs to keep stakeholders abreast of evolving regulations, risk management techniques, and compliance strategies.

5. **Agile Governance Structures:**

   Committee Flexibility: Foster agile governance structures that can adapt swiftly to changes in the business environment. Regular assessments and adjustments are crucial.

6. **Crisis Management:**

   Preparedness: Develop and regularly test crisis management plans to ensure a swift and effective response to unforeseen events.

7. **Regulatory Intelligence Platforms:**

   Automated Updates: Leverage regulatory intelligence platforms for automated updates on changes in regulations, ensuring proactive compliance strategies.

8. **Audit Trail and Reporting Tools:**

   Transparency: Implement audit trail and reporting tools for transparency in compliance activities, aiding in building trust with stakeholders and regulatory bodies.

CHAPTER EIGHT

THE SYNERGY OF COMMUNICATION - BUILDING BRIDGES IN GRC

In the intricate tapestry of Governance, Risk, and Compliance (GRC), the bedrock of success lies in the seamless synergy of communication, a force that transcends silos, bridges gaps, and forges connections across the organizational landscape. This chapter delves into the profound importance of effective communication as the linchpin in the GRC framework, elucidating how it not only facilitates understanding but acts as the catalyst for cohesive governance, risk management, and compliance strategies.

8.1 The Pinnacle of Cohesive Governance

At the summit of organizational governance stands effective communication, the conduit through which strategic decisions are crafted, disseminated, and comprehended. Boards, committees, and executive leadership must engage in transparent and open communication to align organizational objectives with governance structures.

TRANSPARENT DECISION-MAKING PROCESSES

Transparent decision-making processes, communicated clearly to stakeholders, cultivate trust and foster a sense of inclusivity. The dissemination of governance policies, objectives, and ethical guidelines becomes a shared journey, ensuring that every stakeholder comprehends and embraces the organization's governance ethos.

BOARD-MANAGEMENT COLLABORATION

Effective communication acts as the bridge between the board and management, facilitating the exchange of insights, concerns, and strategic visions. Regular, open dialogue ensures that governance decisions are not unilateral but a collaborative effort that draws from the wealth of expertise at all levels.

8.2 Navigating the Landscape of Risk

In the dynamic realm of risk management, communication emerges as the compass guiding organizations through the ever-shifting landscape. Risk, an omnipresent companion, necessitates a network of communication channels to identify, assess, and respond effectively.

RISK IDENTIFICATION AND REPORTING

Communication channels for risk identification and reporting must be robust and accessible. Employees at all levels should feel empowered to communicate potential risks, ensuring that the organization has a comprehensive understanding of its risk landscape.

REAL-TIME RISK COMMUNICATION

In the face of dynamic risks, real-time communication becomes imperative. Automated systems for risk monitoring and reporting enable organizations to receive instant insights, allowing for swift responses and agile risk mitigation strategies.

8.3 The Compliance Connection

Within the compliance domain, communication is not merely a means of conveying rules but a vehicle for cultivating a culture of integrity and adherence.

CLEAR COMMUNICATION OF POLICIES

Organizations must communicate compliance policies clearly and comprehensively to all stakeholders. This ensures that expectations are well-understood, reducing the likelihood of inadvertent violations.

TRAINING INITIATIVES FOR AWARENESS

Communication extends to continuous training initiatives that keep stakeholders informed about changing compliance landscapes. Webinars, workshops, and interactive modules create an environment where compliance is not viewed as a restrictive mandate but as a shared responsibility.

8.4 The Web of Interconnected Communication

In the broader context, the synergy of communication weaves a web of interconnectedness, fostering collaboration between governance, risk management, and compliance functions.

INTEGRATED GRC PLATFORMS

Leveraging integrated GRC platforms ensures that communication is not fragmented but unified. A shared platform facilitates the seamless flow of information between governance, risk, and compliance functions, creating a holistic understanding of the organization's GRC landscape.

REGULAR REPORTING AND ANALYSIS

Regular reporting and analysis mechanisms become the pulse of GRC communication. Dashboards and reports, accessible to key stakeholders, provide insights into GRC activities, fostering a culture of transparency and accountability.

8.5 The Human Element - Soft Skills in GRC Communication

Beyond processes and platforms, the human element remains pivotal. Soft skills in GRC communication become the adhesive that binds the intricate GRC framework.

ACTIVE LISTENING AND FEEDBACK LOOPS

Active listening becomes a cornerstone in GRC communication. Establishing feedback loops ensures that communication is not unidirectional but a dynamic exchange where insights from stakeholders inform ongoing GRC strategies.

CLARITY IN DOCUMENTATION

Clear and concise documentation, whether in governance policies, risk assessments, or compliance guidelines, ensures that information is easily digestible. This clarity minimizes the risk of misinterpretation and promotes a shared understanding of GRC expectations.

8.6 The Resonance of Effective GRC Communication

In conclusion, the synergy of communication stands as the resonant chord in the symphony of Governance, Risk, and Compliance. It is the force that builds bridges, connects stakeholders, and ensures that the GRC journey is not a series of disparate activities but a cohesive, collaborative endeavor. As organizations weave through the complexities of GRC, the mastery of communication becomes not just a skill but a strategic imperative, harmonizing the diverse elements of governance, risk management, and compliance into a symphony of organizational resilience and integrity.

CHAPTER NINE

STRATEGIC THINKING: THE CORNERSTONE OF GRC EXCELLENCE

Coming off the back of synergy of communication in GRC, it then becomes important to discuss the importance of strategic thinking and how it is the pillar that guarantees excellence in GRC.

In Governance, Risk, and Compliance (GRC), strategic thinking stands as the cornerstone, the invisible force that weaves coherence into the fabric of organizational excellence. It is the mindset that transcends the conventional, viewing GRC not as isolated functions but as interconnected elements of a holistic strategy.

Strategic thinking in GRC entails aligning governance, risk management, and compliance with the overarching objectives of the organization. It anticipates risks before they materialize, embracing a proactive stance that safeguards the organization against uncertainties. It fosters the development of agile governance structures, capable of adapting to the dynamic business environment without compromising on accountability.

Moreover, strategic thinking sees compliance as more than a checklist; it transforms it into a strategic advantage. It integrates compliance frameworks with the organization's strategic goals, making adherence to regulations a proactive strategy rather than a reactive necessity.

Data-driven decision-making becomes a hallmark of strategic thinking in GRC. By harnessing the power of data analytics, organizations gain empirical insights into governance effectiveness, risk trends, and compliance performance. This informed decision-making ensures that GRC activities are not based on assumptions but on a foundation of tangible evidence.

Strategic thinking cultivates a GRC culture, permeating every stakeholder with an understanding of the strategic importance of governance, the proactive nature of risk management, and the value of compliance in achieving organizational objectives. It breaks down silos between GRC functions, fostering collaboration and communication, creating an integrated framework where these functions operate synergistically.

Acknowledging the dynamic nature of regulatory environments, strategic thinking in GRC crafts strategies that can adapt swiftly to changes in regulations. Compliance becomes an integral part of a strategic approach to risk mitigation and governance, ensuring that it is not a burdensome reaction but an essential element of the organizational strategy.

The elements of strategic thinking includeS an analysis of critical situations and complex scenarios, a clear vision of long-term goals coupled with a clear roadmap, constant monitoring of changing market trends and technical progress, and competition (Goswami, 2023). In GRC, it is an ongoing mindset, not a one-time exercise. It views continuous improvement as a strategic imperative, regularly reassessing and refining GRC strategies based on lessons learned, changing business environments, and emerging risks. It is the compass that guides GRC activities toward excellence, ensuring that governance, risk management, and compliance are not just functions but integral components of a cohesive and forward-thinking organizational strategy.

A more structured breakdown is given below:

I. **Holistic Alignment of Objectives**

Strategic thinking in GRC involves aligning governance, risk management, and compliance with the overarching objectives of the organization. It ensures that each element of GRC is not viewed in isolation but as integral components of a unified strategy aimed at achieving organizational goals.

II. **Proactive Risk Anticipation and Mitigation**

Strategic thinking anticipates risks before they crystallize into threats. It involves a forward-looking approach to risk management, identifying potential pitfalls and proactively devising mitigation strategies. By embedding risk considerations into strategic planning, organizations become resilient in the face of uncertainties.

III. **Agile Governance Structures**

Strategic thinking fosters the development of agile governance structures that can adapt to the dynamic business environment. It involves crafting governance models that are not rigid but flexible, allowing for swift adjustments in response to changing circumstances without compromising on accountability and ethical standards.

IV. **Integration of Compliance as a Strategic Advantage**

Compliance is not merely a checklist but a strategic advantage when viewed through the lens of strategic thinking. It involves aligning compliance frameworks with the organization's strategic objectives, ensuring that adherence to regulations becomes a proactive strategy rather than a reactive necessity.

V. **Data-Driven Decision-Making**

Strategic thinking leverages data-driven decision-making in the GRC landscape. It involves harnessing the power of data analytics to gain insights into governance effectiveness, risk trends, and compliance performance. This informed decision-making ensures that GRC activities are not based on assumptions but on empirical evidence.

VI. Long-Term Resilience

Strategic thinking extends beyond short-term goals, focusing on building long-term resilience. It involves crafting GRC strategies that consider the sustainability of governance structures, the adaptability of risk management frameworks, and the enduring relevance of compliance practices in the ever-evolving regulatory landscape.

vii. Integration of GRC Functions

Strategic thinking breaks down silos between governance, risk, and compliance functions, fostering collaboration and communication. It involves creating an integrated GRC framework where these functions operate synergistically, sharing insights, and collectively contributing to the organization's success.

VII. Cultivation of a GRC Culture

Strategic thinking is instrumental in cultivating a GRC culture within the organization. It involves instilling a mindset where every stakeholder, from the board to employees at all levels, understands the strategic importance of governance, the proactive nature of risk management, and the value of compliance in achieving organizational objectives.

VIII. Adaptation to Changing Regulatory Landscapes

Strategic thinking acknowledges the dynamic nature of regulatory environments. It involves creating GRC strategies that can adapt swiftly to changes in regulations, ensuring that compliance is not a burdensome reaction but an integral part of a strategic approach to risk mitigation and governance.

IX. Continuous Improvement as a Strategic Imperative

Strategic thinking views continuous improvement as a strategic imperative. It involves regularly reassessing and refining GRC strategies based on lessons learned, changing business environments, and emerging risks. This iterative approach ensures that GRC practices remain not just effective but continually optimized.

In essence, strategic thinking in GRC is not a one-time exercise but an ongoing mindset that permeates every facet of organizational decision-making. It is the compass that guides GRC activities toward excellence, ensuring that governance, risk management, and compliance are not isolated functions but integral components of a cohesive and forward-thinking organizational strategy.

9.1 Problem-Solving Paradigm: GRC Edition

In the intricate tapestry of Governance, Risk, and Compliance (GRC), the 'Problem-Solving Paradigm' emerges as the guiding principle, illuminating the path towards effective decision-making and organizational resilience. This paradigm encapsulates the essence of strategic thinking and adaptability, acknowledging that challenges within the GRC landscape are not roadblocks but opportunities for innovation and improvement.

At its core, the Problem-Solving Paradigm in GRC underscores the importance of a proactive approach. Rather than viewing issues as isolated incidents, organizations adopting this paradigm recognize them as integral components of the dynamic business environment. It involves cultivating a mindset that anticipates challenges, identifies root causes, and devises strategic solutions that go beyond mere firefighting.

Strategic problem-solving in GRC is deeply intertwined with governance structures. It involves not only addressing issues as they arise but also preemptively fortifying governance frameworks to mitigate potential risks. Leaders become architects of robust governance systems, constantly reassessing and refining them to align with the ever-evolving organizational landscape.

Risk, an inherent companion in business, finds its place in the Problem-Solving Paradigm through proactive risk management. Rather than treating risks as unavoidable hindrances, organizations employing this paradigm approach them as navigable terrains. Risk assessments become dynamic tools, providing insights into emerging threats and guiding the formulation of agile risk mitigation strategies.

Moreover, compliance challenges are not viewed in isolation but as integral aspects of the GRC problem-solving landscape. The paradigm involves the integration of compliance initiatives with organizational strategy, transforming compliance from a reactive response to regulatory mandates into a proactive strategic advantage.

The Problem-Solving Paradigm in GRC necessitates a departure from traditional, siloed approaches. It encourages cross-functional collaboration, breaking down barriers between governance, risk, and compliance functions. This collaborative spirit fosters a holistic understanding of challenges, allowing organizations to formulate comprehensive solutions that address the interconnected nature of GRC issues.

Technology plays a pivotal role within this paradigm, serving as an enabler rather than a panacea. Integrated GRC platforms become instrumental tools, providing real-time insights, facilitating data-driven decision-making, and streamlining processes. However, the human element remains paramount, with the paradigm recognizing the importance of soft skills such as communication, adaptability, and critical thinking in effective problem-solving.

In conclusion, the 'Problem-Solving Paradigm: GRC Edition' represents a shift in mindset and approach, positioning challenges not as obstacles but as opportunities for growth and innovation. Organizations embracing this paradigm view problem-solving as a continuous, adaptive process ingrained in the very fabric of their GRC culture. Through strategic governance, proactive risk management, and an integrated approach to compliance, they navigate the GRC landscape with resilience and ingenuity, ensuring that challenges become stepping stones toward organizational excellence.

9.2 Collaboration Chronicles: GRC in a Team Context

Within the dynamic landscape of Governance, Risk, and Compliance (GRC), the 'Collaboration Chronicles' unfold as a narrative that underscores the transformative power of teamwork in shaping a resilient and effective GRC framework. It is a tale of cross-functional collaboration, where individuals from diverse backgrounds unite their strengths, forging a collective force that transcends silos and propels organizations towards GRC excellence.

In the context of GRC, the Collaboration Chronicles signify a departure from isolated endeavors towards a culture of interconnectedness. It is a recognition that governance, risk management, and compliance are not standalone functions but interwoven threads that collectively contribute to the fabric of organizational success. Through collaborative efforts, stakeholders engage in a shared journey where the synergy of their diverse skills and perspectives becomes a strategic advantage.

Governance, as depicted in the Collaboration Chronicles, becomes a collective responsibility. Boards, executives, and management collaborate transparently, ensuring that decision-making processes are not confined to hierarchical structures but draw from the collective wisdom of the team. It involves fostering an environment where governance is not merely a set of rules but a dynamic dialogue that reflects the collective values and aspirations of the organization.

Risk management, within the collaborative narrative, transforms into a team effort. Rather than relying solely on risk experts, organizations harness the insights of individuals from various departments. This cross-functional collaboration enables a comprehensive understanding of risks, facilitates real-time risk identification, and empowers teams to craft adaptive risk mitigation strategies that align with organizational objectives.

Compliance, as woven into the Collaboration Chronicles, evolves beyond a checklist mentality. It involves a collective commitment to adhering to regulatory standards, where compliance officers, legal teams, and operational staff collaborate seamlessly. Through shared communication channels and a united understanding of compliance requirements, organizations ensure that compliance is not a burdensome task but an integral part of their collective responsibility.

Technology becomes an enabler in the Collaboration Chronicles, providing integrated GRC platforms that serve as the collaborative hub. These platforms facilitate real-time information sharing, streamline communication, and offer a centralized space for collaborative decision-making. However, the Chronicles recognize that technology is a tool wielded by the hands of a collaborative team, emphasizing the human element in utilizing these advancements.

Soft skills take center stage in the Collaboration Chronicles. Effective communication, active listening, and the ability to work collectively become the linchpins of successful GRC collaboration. Teams foster an environment where diverse perspectives are valued, and every stakeholder has a voice in the GRC dialogue.

In sum, the 'Collaboration Chronicles: GRC in a Team Context' tell a story of shared responsibility, collective wisdom, and the transformative power of teamwork. It is an ode to the idea that GRC is not a solo performance but a symphony where each instrument plays a unique role, contributing to the harmonious governance, resilient risk management, and proactive compliance that define organizational success. Through collaboration, organizations script a narrative where GRC is not a set of tasks but a collective journey towards excellence.

9.3 The Art of Adaptability: GRC in a Dynamic World

In the ever-evolving landscape of Governance, Risk, and Compliance (GRC), 'The Art of Adaptability' emerges as a defining ethos, illuminating the path to success in a dynamic and unpredictable world. It is a narrative that underscores the paramount importance of agility and resilience in navigating the complexities of GRC, where change is not a challenge but an opportunity for innovation and growth.

At its core, 'The Art of Adaptability: GRC in a Dynamic World' encapsulates the understanding that the only constant in the GRC realm is change. It recognizes that governance structures, risk landscapes, and compliance requirements are fluid entities, shaped by external forces such as regulatory shifts, technological advancements, and global economic trends. In response, organizations embracing this narrative cultivate a mindset that views adaptability not as a contingency plan but as an inherent strength.

Governance, within the realm of adaptability, transforms into a flexible framework capable of swift adjustments. Boards and executives foster an environment where governance structures are not static blueprints but living entities that can adapt to emerging challenges. The art lies in crafting governance models that balance stability with flexibility, ensuring that they remain resilient in the face of dynamic business environments.

Risk management, as depicted in the narrative, becomes a proactive and anticipatory endeavor. Rather than reacting to risks as they materialize, organizations employing the art of adaptability engage in continuous risk assessment. This involves leveraging data analytics, scenario planning, and real-time monitoring to identify and address risks before they escalate. The art lies in creating risk management strategies that are not only robust but agile in response to the evolving risk landscape.

Compliance, woven into the adaptability narrative, evolves beyond a reactive stance to regulatory changes. It involves the art of staying ahead of compliance requirements, anticipating shifts in the regulatory landscape, and integrating compliance initiatives seamlessly into organizational strategies. The art lies in viewing compliance not as a static set of rules but as a dynamic process that aligns with the ever-changing regulatory environment.

Technology becomes an ally in the art of adaptability, providing organizations with tools for real-time data analysis, automation of repetitive tasks, and the integration of GRC functions. However, the narrative emphasizes that technology is not a one-size-fits-all solution but a customizable tool that organizations wield to enhance their adaptive capabilities.

Soft skills take center stage in 'The Art of Adaptability,' where effective communication, collaboration, and a culture of continuous learning become essential components. Teams cultivate an environment where adaptability is not merely a skill but a shared value, permeating every level of the organization.

In conclusion, 'The Art of Adaptability: GRC in a Dynamic World' narrates a story of organizational resilience, where adaptability is not a survival strategy but a core competency. It is a narrative that celebrates change as an integral part of the GRC journey, where the art lies in embracing uncertainties with a proactive and innovative spirit. Through adaptability, organizations not only navigate the dynamic GRC landscape but thrive in an environment where change is not a hindrance but a catalyst for sustained success.

9.4 Risk Management Resonance: Non-Tech Strategies

In the orchestration of effective Risk Management, a symphony of strategies unfolds, transcending technological solutions. This narrative, titled 'Risk Management Resonance: Non-Tech Strategies,' delves into the non-technological dimensions that echo with significance in the complex realm of risk management. It articulates a melody where human-centric approaches, strategic planning, and organizational culture harmonize to create a resilient and proactive risk management framework.

At its essence, 'Risk Management Resonance' underscores the notion that effective risk management is not solely reliant on technology but is deeply intertwined with human intuition, strategic foresight, and a pervasive risk-aware culture.

Human-Centric Approaches take center stage in this narrative. It delves into the importance of cultivating a risk-aware mindset among employees at all levels. Through training, awareness programs, and a commitment to open communication, organizations can tap into the collective intelligence of their workforce. This human-centric approach transforms every employee into a risk sentinel, contributing to the early identification and mitigation of potential risks.

Strategic Planning emerges as a key non-technological pillar in the resonance of risk management. It involves the art of foresight, where organizations anticipate and prepare for potential risks before they materialize. Strategic planning includes scenario analysis, trend forecasting, and developing contingency plans. This non-tech strategy positions organizations to navigate uncertainties with agility and precision.

Organizational Culture becomes a fundamental element in risk management resonance. A culture that values transparency, accountability, and ethical behavior creates an environment where individuals feel empowered to raise concerns and report potential risks. This culture of openness forms an integral part of risk identification, as employees become more attuned to recognizing and addressing risks in their respective areas.

Leadership Engagement is paramount in the non-tech symphony of risk management. Leaders set the tone for risk-awareness, actively participating in risk discussions, and fostering a culture where risk management is not solely a function of specialized teams but a shared responsibility. Leadership engagement also includes providing clear guidance on risk tolerance and promoting a balance between risk-taking and risk aversion.

Collaboration and Communication weave into the fabric of risk management resonance. Effective collaboration breaks down silos, ensuring that information flows seamlessly across departments. Non-tech communication strategies, such as regular risk briefings, town hall meetings, and interactive workshops, enhance the understanding of risk management principles among stakeholders.

Training and Development serve as non-tech instruments that enhance the skills and capabilities of employees in the realm of risk management. From basic risk awareness training for all staff to specialized courses for risk management professionals, continuous learning ensures that the workforce is equipped to navigate the complexities of the risk landscape.

To cap, 'Risk Management Resonance: Non-Tech Strategies' is a narrative that celebrates the multifaceted nature of risk management. It acknowledges that while technology is a valuable tool, the resonance of effective risk management emanates from human-centric approaches, strategic planning, organizational culture, leadership engagement, collaboration, communication, and ongoing training. It is a melody where each non-tech element contributes to the harmonious orchestration of a robust risk management framework, ensuring organizations navigate uncertainties with a resonance that echoes with foresight, adaptability, and organizational resilience.

CHAPTER TEN

FROM INSIGHT TO ACTION: LEVERAGING YOUR UNIQUE GRC SKILL SET

Strategic thinking can be the pillar that will firmly support GRC's excellence but it is the crucial step of translating insights into action that will be the most defining.

As you venture into Governance, Risk, and Compliance (GRC), the narrative of 'From Insight to Action: Leveraging Your Unique GRC Skill Set' unfolds as a compelling journey of transformation. It is an invitation for individuals within the GRC domain to not only possess insights but to harness and deploy their unique skill sets for proactive and impactful contributions to organizational success.

At its essence, 'From Insight to Action' encapsulates the idea that possessing knowledge in GRC is not enough; it is the application of this knowledge that propels organizations forward. It is a narrative that encourages GRC professionals to become architects of change, leveraging their distinct skills to drive strategic initiatives and foster a culture of excellence.

The unique GRC skill set encompasses a multifaceted range of capabilities:

1. **Analytical Prowess**

   GRC professionals possess the ability to analyze complex data sets, trends, and scenarios. 'From Insight to Action' emphasizes the transformation of analytical insights into tangible strategies. This involves translating data-driven findings into actionable plans that enhance governance structures, mitigate risks, and ensure compliance.

Analytical prowess is a guiding force that steers professionals through the complexities of decision-making and strategic planning. It is the art of systematically dissecting information, unraveling patterns, and extracting meaningful insights that underpin the fabric of effective GRC practices.

Within the realm of GRC, analytical skills find a profound application in the assessment of risks. Professionals adept in analytical prowess engage in a meticulous evaluation of potential risks, weighing their likelihood and impact. This analytical lens allows for the prioritization of risks, ensuring that attention is directed to the most significant threats facing the organization.

Data, often voluminous and diverse, is a cornerstone of GRC efforts. Analytical acumen equips professionals to navigate this sea of information, employing data analysis tools to distill actionable insights. Through this lens, trends emerge, and decisions become grounded in the empirical evidence drawn from thorough data analysis.

Navigating the intricate web of regulatory compliance demands a keen analytical eye. GRC professionals use their analytical prowess to interpret and dissect complex regulatory frameworks, ensuring organizational activities align seamlessly with the ever-evolving landscape of laws and standards.

Scenario modeling, a strategic exercise in anticipating the potential outcomes of diverse situations, is enriched by analytical skills. Professionals leverage their ability to analyze various scenarios, providing organizations with a foresight that empowers them to proactively address risks and challenges.

When issues arise, analytical skills shine in the realm of root cause analysis. GRC professionals delve into the intricacies of problems, unraveling the underlying factors that contribute to issues. This deep dive enables them to address challenges at their source, fostering sustainable solutions.

Decision support, a critical function in GRC, thrives on analytical prowess. Professionals analyze complex situations, weighing the implications of different decisions. Armed with insights, they provide decision-makers with a foundation of data-driven knowledge, facilitating well-informed choices.

Trend analysis becomes a dynamic tool in the GRC toolkit, powered by analytical capabilities. Professionals discern patterns within data, identifying trends that inform strategic decisions. This proactive approach ensures organizations stay ahead of emerging issues.

In defining and monitoring Key Performance Indicators (KPIs), analytical skills play a pivotal role. GRC professionals employ data analysis to measure the effectiveness of governance structures, risk management processes, and compliance initiatives, fostering a culture of continuous improvement.

Audit and assurance processes benefit immensely from analytical prowess. GRC professionals use their analytical skills to scrutinize financial and operational data, assess internal controls, and ensure alignment with established policies and procedures.

In the forward-looking realm of GRC, predictive analytics becomes a visionary tool. Professionals leverage historical data and statistical models to forecast potential risks and compliance challenges, enabling organizations to take preemptive actions.

2. **Effective Communication**

Communication emerges as a linchpin in the narrative, recognizing that the ability to convey complex GRC concepts to diverse stakeholders is a powerful skill. GRC professionals become storytellers, articulating the importance of governance, explaining risk implications, and elucidating the significance of compliance in a language that resonates throughout the organization.

Effective communication serves as the masterstroke that weaves together the diverse threads of understanding, collaboration, and transparency. It is the cornerstone upon which the intricate decisions and complexities of GRC find resonance. Here's how effective communication unfolds within the realms of GRC:

Within the governance structures of an organization, effective communication acts as a beacon of clarity. It illuminates roles, responsibilities, and reporting lines, ensuring a shared comprehension of the mechanisms through which decisions are conceived and executed.

Transparent communication becomes the bedrock of risk discussions. GRC professionals articulate and discuss risks openly, cultivating trust among stakeholders and creating a collective awareness of potential challenges that might lie ahead.

Guiding individuals through compliance requirements hinges on effective communication. GRC professionals convey policies, procedures, and regulatory changes with clarity, offering guidance and educational resources that facilitate adherence and understanding.

In the realm of reporting and documentation, effective communication is a craft. GRC professionals present information clearly and concisely, ensuring that reports are not just data but narratives that facilitate informed decision-making, transparency, and accountability.

During crises, the art of effective communication becomes a lifeline. GRC professionals communicate swiftly and accurately to internal and external stakeholders, providing updates, addressing concerns, and outlining mitigation strategies with a clarity that instills confidence.

Stakeholder engagement, a pivotal aspect of GRC, relies on effective communication. GRC professionals actively listen to stakeholders, address their concerns, and keep them informed about governance decisions, risk management strategies, and compliance initiatives, building a collaborative and informed community.

Engaging with boards and executives demands a special kind of communication finesse. GRC professionals convey complex information in a manner that resonates with leadership, ensuring that key decision-makers are well-informed and can make strategic choices aligned with organizational objectives.

Training programs and awareness initiatives in GRC thrive on effective communication. GRC professionals articulate the importance of governance structures, explain risk management protocols, and clarify compliance obligations, ensuring that employees are well-versed and aligned with organizational goals.

Cross-functional collaboration, a hallmark of effective GRC, relies on communication that transcends departmental boundaries. GRC professionals facilitate seamless information flow, breaking down silos and ensuring that teams work in concert toward common objectives.

Navigating cultural nuances is an art within globalized GRC, and effective communication is the brushstroke. GRC professionals tailor their communication strategies to resonate with diverse audiences, fostering a shared understanding of governance principles and compliance expectations across cultural spectrums.

In the digital age, effective communication in GRC embraces technology and platforms. GRC professionals leverage communication tools to disseminate information, collaborate in real-time, and ensure that updates reach stakeholders in a timely and efficient manner.

3. Strategic Thinking

Strategic thinking is celebrated as a cornerstone skill in the journey from insight to action. GRC professionals are encouraged to not only identify risks but to think strategically about how these risks align with organizational objectives. This involves developing proactive risk management strategies and aligning governance practices with long-term strategic goals.

Strategic thinking can be perceived as the compass guiding professionals toward a future-oriented and comprehensive approach. It is a mindset that extends beyond immediate challenges, envisioning plans that not only address current issues but also anticipate and navigate potential obstacles on the horizon. Here's how strategic thinking unfolds within the realms of GRC:

Strategic thinkers in GRC embark on crafting visionary governance structures. It's not merely about addressing present needs; it involves developing frameworks that can adapt to future changes in the business environment and the ever-evolving regulatory landscape.

Anticipation and mitigation of risks take center stage in the strategic thinking playbook. Professionals engage in proactive scenario planning, identifying potential threats and devising strategies to preemptively mitigate risks, safeguarding the organization's interests.

Far from viewing compliance as a mere obligation, strategic thinkers perceive it as a competitive advantage. They align compliance efforts with broader organizational objectives, leveraging adherence to regulatory standards to enhance reputation, build trust, and position the organization strategically in the market.

The integration of GRC into the broader business strategy is a hallmark of strategic thinking. GRC professionals ensure that governance, risk management, and compliance initiatives seamlessly align with and contribute to the achievement of the organization's strategic goals.

Performance metrics underpinning strategic GRC are not mere data points; they are carefully crafted indicators aligned with strategic objectives. Key Performance Indicators (KPIs) measure the effectiveness of governance structures, risk management processes, and compliance initiatives in achieving organizational goals.

Acknowledging the dynamic nature of risks, strategic GRC professionals develop adaptive risk management strategies. These strategies evolve with changing business environments, ensuring the organization remains resilient in the face of emerging challenges.

Collaborative decision-making is woven into the fabric of strategic GRC. Engaging key stakeholders, including executives, boards, and cross-functional teams, in strategic discussions ensures a holistic and informed approach to decision-making.

The culture of continuous improvement is a cornerstone of strategic GRC. Regular assessments of governance, risk management, and compliance initiatives identify areas for enhancement, allowing the organization to adapt to growth and industry changes.

Leveraging technology as an enabler for GRC is a strategic move. Strategic thinkers explore and integrate technological solutions that enhance the efficiency of governance structures, facilitate risk assessments, and streamline compliance processes.

Training and development programs under the strategic thinking umbrella are future-focused. GRC professionals ensure that employees are equipped not only for current compliance but also for future challenges, fostering a culture of continuous learning and adaptability.

Stakeholder engagement is not a one-time interaction; it's part of a comprehensive strategy. Strategic GRC professionals communicate with internal and external stakeholders in a way that aligns with organizational objectives, building trust and collaboration that extends beyond immediate concerns.

4. **Change Management Expertise**

In a dynamic GRC landscape, change is inevitable. 'From Insight to Action' acknowledges the skill of managing change effectively. GRC professionals become catalysts for change, guiding organizations through shifts in regulatory environments, technological advancements, and evolving risk landscapes with a focus on adaptability and resilience.

Possessing change management expertise is akin to holding the compass that guides organizations through the intricate terrain of evolving structures and frameworks. This proficiency involves a strategic understanding of the need for change in governance, risk management, and compliance, coupled with the ability to lead stakeholders seamlessly through the transition. Here's how change management expertise manifests in the context of GRC:

Change management experts in GRC begin by assessing the need for transformation. They meticulously analyze the current state of governance, risk management, and compliance, identifying areas that necessitate adjustment to align with shifting business objectives and regulatory landscapes.

Thorough stakeholder analyses form a cornerstone of change management expertise. GRC professionals identify key stakeholders, assess their interests, and craft tailored engagement strategies to garner support and effectively manage any resistance to changes in the GRC landscape.

Crafting a compelling vision for the future state is another hallmark of change management proficiency. GRC leaders articulate how alterations in governance, risk management, and compliance will contribute to the overarching success of the organization, instilling a sense of purpose and direction among stakeholders.

Effective communication strategies take center stage. Change management experts develop and implement communication plans that convey the rationale behind GRC changes, address concerns, and keep stakeholders informed throughout the transition process.

Building a culture that is ready for change is a key focus. Change management expertise in GRC involves fostering an environment where adaptability and resilience are valued, ensuring that teams are prepared to embrace new governance structures, risk management practices, and compliance requirements.

Change impact assessments precede implementation. GRC professionals evaluate how changes will ripple through existing processes, roles, and workflows, identifying and mitigating potential risks to ensure a smooth transition.

Training and development programs are designed and implemented. GRC leaders ensure that employees acquire the necessary skills and knowledge to navigate within the new GRC framework, facilitating a seamless transition.

Monitoring and adapting to feedback are ongoing processes. Change management experts establish feedback loops, attentively listening to concerns and suggestions, and adapt change strategies accordingly to refine the transition based on real-time insights.

Aligning changes with organizational values is integral. GRC professionals ensure that revised governance, risk, and compliance frameworks resonate with the core values of the organization, promoting cohesion and harmony during the transition.

Celebrating milestones and successes becomes a ritual. Change leaders in GRC acknowledge the achievements of teams and individuals, reinforcing a positive narrative around the changes and motivating stakeholders to embrace further adaptations.

Continuous improvement is the guiding principle. Change management experts foster a culture of ongoing enhancement, analyzing outcomes, identifying areas for improvement, and iterating on the change management process to ensure sustained success in the evolving landscape of GRC.

5. Collaboration and Relationship Building

The narrative places a spotlight on the collaborative nature of GRC work. GRC professionals are encouraged to build strong relationships across departments, fostering a culture where GRC is not viewed as a siloed function but an integrated and collaborative effort. Collaboration becomes a tool for translating insights into actionable plans that resonate throughout the organization.

The significance of collaboration and relationship building is portrayed as a foundational narrative weaving through the fabric of governance structures, risk management, and compliance frameworks. It is a nuanced orchestration, entailing the art of forging connections, nurturing communication, and building partnerships across the diverse spectrum of organizational landscapes. Here's how the symphony of collaboration and relationship building resonates within the context of GRC:

Interdepartmental Collaboration becomes the heartbeat of GRC, dismantling silos as professionals collaborate seamlessly with departments such as legal, finance, and IT, fostering a holistic approach to governance, risk management, and compliance.

Stakeholder Engagement transcends transactional interactions, evolving into a dynamic process where GRC professionals actively listen to the concerns and expectations of internal and external stakeholders. This approach cultivates a collaborative environment enriched by diverse perspectives.

Cross-Functional Teams form a nexus of expertise, embodying collaborative efforts to address complex challenges. GRC professionals adeptly build and lead cross-functional teams, harnessing the collective knowledge of individuals from various disciplines.

Board and Executive Engagement become pivotal as GRC professionals cultivate relationships with leadership. They provide insights, present reports, and offer strategic recommendations, ensuring a symbiotic relationship that aligns with organizational objectives and risk appetite.

Vendor and Third-Party Relationships extend collaboration beyond organizational boundaries. GRC professionals carefully build and manage relationships with external entities, ensuring compliance standards are met and fostering positive contributions to overall risk management.

Regulatory Relationships take center stage as GRC professionals establish open lines of communication with regulatory bodies. This collaborative approach facilitates transparency and a cooperative spirit in meeting compliance requirements.

Training and Awareness Programs are collaborative initiatives aimed at building knowledge within the organization. GRC professionals collaborate with HR and training departments, developing programs to educate employees on governance principles, risk awareness, and compliance requirements.

Communication Networks become the conduits of collaboration. GRC professionals leverage communication tools to facilitate real-time information exchange, ensuring stakeholders are well-informed about changes in governance, risk profiles, and compliance standards.

Conflict Resolution becomes an art within the collaborative landscape of GRC. Professionals navigate and resolve conflicts arising from differing views on risk appetite, compliance interpretations, or governance structures, ensuring a harmonious working environment.

Continuous Feedback Loops characterize the collaborative spirit in GRC. Professionals actively seek input from stakeholders, fostering a culture where feedback is valued and used to refine governance structures, risk management processes, and compliance initiatives.

Community and Industry Collaboration extend the collaborative ethos beyond organizational boundaries. GRC professionals build relationships within broader industry and professional communities, sharing best practices and staying informed about industry trends.

In essence, collaboration and relationship building in GRC are not mere strategies; they are the heartbeat of a thriving ecosystem. They constitute the interconnected narratives that fortify governance foundations, navigate risks, and ensure compliance resonates across every facet of the organization's landscape. This collaborative symphony, when conducted skillfully, contributes to the holistic success and resilience of the organization in the dynamic tapestry of GRC.

6. **Leadership Acumen**

Leadership skills are highlighted as instrumental in the journey from insight to action. GRC professionals are called upon to lead by example, championing the importance of governance, risk management, and compliance at all levels of the organization. Leadership acumen involves inspiring others to embrace GRC principles as integral components of their roles.

Leadership acumen is the cornerstone, guiding organizations through the labyrinth of governance structures, risk management intricacies, and compliance frameworks. It embodies a unique amalgamation of strategic vision, adept decision-making, and the ability to inspire and guide teams through the complexities of GRC. Here's how leadership acumen weaves its narrative in the realm of GRC:

Leadership in GRC requires a Strategic Vision that aligns the intricate threads of governance, risk management, and compliance with the broader organizational objectives. Leaders envision a GRC framework that not only addresses current needs but anticipates and adapts to future challenges.

Decisiveness is a hallmark of leadership acumen in GRC. Leaders exhibit agility in decision-making, navigating through complex risk scenarios, interpreting evolving regulatory landscapes, and making informed decisions that harmonize compliance requirements with the strategic goals of the organization.

Stakeholder Management is a key facet of effective leadership in GRC. Leaders adeptly build and nurture relationships with internal and external stakeholders, ensuring alignment and collaboration in governance initiatives and compliance efforts.

Leaders in GRC assume the role of Risk Navigators. They provide direction in assessing, prioritizing, and mitigating risks, understanding that effective risk management is integral to the organization's overall resilience and success.

Regulatory Navigation is a skill of leadership acumen in GRC. Leaders stay well-informed about evolving regulations, interpret their implications, and guide the organization in maintaining compliance while leveraging regulatory changes strategically.

Leaders foster a culture of Collaboration and Team Building within GRC teams. They build diverse, cross-functional teams, encouraging open communication and collaboration to address challenges and implement effective governance and compliance measures.

Adaptive Innovation is embraced by leaders in GRC. They encourage the use of technology and data analytics to enhance governance structures, streamline compliance processes, and improve the efficiency of risk management initiatives.

Ethical Leadership is fundamental to GRC. Leaders set a tone of integrity and ethical conduct, emphasizing the importance of compliance not just as a requirement but as a fundamental aspect of organizational values.

Change Management Proficiency is part of leadership acumen in GRC. Leaders guide the organization through changes in governance practices, compliance requirements, and risk management strategies, ensuring a smooth transition and buy-in from stakeholders.

Continuous Learning and Development are commitments of GRC leaders. They stay abreast of industry trends, emerging risks, and advancements in governance and compliance practices, fostering a culture of learning and development within GRC teams.

Communication Excellence is a hallmark of leadership acumen in GRC. Leaders communicate complex governance and compliance concepts in a clear and understandable manner, ensuring that stakeholders are well-informed and aligned with organizational objectives.

Resilient Leadership characterizes the leadership acumen in GRC. Leaders navigate uncertainties, adapt to changing landscapes, and instill a sense of confidence and stability within the organization, fostering a resilient GRC framework.

In conclusion, 'From Insight to Action: Leveraging Your Unique GRC Skill Set' is an empowering narrative that urges GRC professionals to be catalysts for change within their organizations. It is a journey that transcends theoretical knowledge, calling upon individuals to apply their analytical prowess, effective communication, strategic thinking, change management expertise, collaboration skills, and leadership acumen to translate GRC insights into actions that drive organizational success. It is an invitation to not only understand the intricacies of GRC but to actively shape and influence the GRC landscape with a skill set that is uniquely poised for impactful contributions.

REFERENCES

- Anwari, Farhad. "From Zero to GRC Hero: Your Guide to a Thrilling Career in Cybersecurity Governance." Medium, Medium, 13 Feb. 2023, medium.com/@farhadanwari58/from-zero-to-grc-hero-your-guide-to-a-thrilling-career-in-cybersecurity-governance-ca888dd8f6fe. Accessed 17 Nov. 2023.
- Appazov, Artur. Legal Aspects of Cybersecurity. 2014.
- "Customer Trust 101: A Primer for Security & GRC Leaders - SafeBase Blog." Safebase.io, safebase.io/blog/customer-trust-101-a-primer-for-security-grc-leaders. Accessed 17 Nov. 2023.
- "Cybersecurity Ethics." DC Encompass, 25 July 2021, dcencompass.com.au/blog/cybersecurity-ethics/.
- Goswami, Kamolika. A Concise Guide to Strategic Thinking. 2023, study.com/learn/lesson/strategic-thinking-definition-purpose-examples.html. Accessed 17 Nov. 2023.
- Longbottom, Clive, and Rob Bamforth. Governance, Risk Management and Compliance (GRC) Dealing with GRC in an Increasingly Complex Information -Centric World. 2013.
- Majoub, Abdullah. "How to Get Started in Cybersecurity GRC without an IT or CS Background."Www.linkedin.com, 13 Aug. 2023, www.linkedin.com/pulse/how-get-started-cybersecurity-grc-without-cs-abdullah-mahjoub?utm_source=rss&utm_campaign=articles_sitemaps. Accessed 17 Nov. 2023.
- OECD. Risk Management and Corporate Governance. Corporate Governance, OECD, 1 Apr. 2014.
- PWC. Governance, Risk Management and Compliance: Sustainability and Integration Supported by Technology. 2004, www.pwc.com.au/consulting/assets/risk-controls/governance_mar09.pdf.

- Steinberg, Richard M. Governance, Risk Management, and Compliance : It Can't Happen to Us-Avoiding Corporate Disaster While Driving Success. Hoboken, N.J., Wiley, 2011.
- The World Bank. "Data Protection and Privacy Laws | Identification for Development." Id4d.worldbank.org, 2023, id4d.worldbank.org/guide/data-protection-and-privacy-laws.

ABOUT THE AUTHOR

The Author, Tolulope Michael, is a proud Computer Science graduate from the esteemed and prestigious Lagos State University. His love for technology, combined with a strong interest in cybersecurity, has driven him to dedicate close to two decades of his life to this field.

Over the years, he has gained valuable experience in various domains of cybersecurity, including Penetration Testing, Application Security Engineering, Cloud Security Engineering, and Governance, Risk and Compliance (GRC). He is proud to say that he has contributed to the growth of the industry, leaving a lasting impact with his expertise and knowledge.

In his quest to help others succeed in cybersecurity, he created ExcelMindCyber, a platform designed to provide comprehensive education in this field. His flagship program, "The Ultimate Cybersecurity Program" has already made a significant impact, helping many individuals realize their potential and earn multiple six figures.

He is grateful for the opportunity to share his passion and knowledge with others, and it brings him immense joy to see his students find success and fulfillment in this field. His journey in cybersecurity has been a rewarding one, and he is proud to be a part of this industry. He hopes to continue making a difference in the lives of those who share his love for cybersecurity, and is committed to helping them achieve their goals. This is his story, and he is proud to tell it.

With a clear and accessible writing style, he provides a roadmap for individuals looking to break into the field of cybersecurity, offering practical advice and actionable tips that will help you succeed in your journey. Whether you're a student, a professional looking for a change, or simply someone with an interest in cybersecurity, the author's insights and guidance will help you build the foundation you need for an exciting and rewarding career.

www.ingramcontent.com/pod-product-compliance
Lightning Source LLC
LaVergne TN
LVHW050930210926
848482LV00013B/597

* 9 7 9 8 9 8 9 6 0 9 9 0 1 *